This belongs to

A Day At A Time

Daily Readings for Men

Richard Halverson

ZONDERVAN
PUBLISHING HOUSE

OF THE ZONDERVAN CORPORATION | GRAND RAPIDS MICHIGAN 49506

A Day at a Time

Copyright © 1974 by The Zondervan Corporation
Grand Rapids, Michigan
Library of Congress Catalog Card Number: 74-11851

Sixth printing   October 1977

Printed in the United States of America

Catalog Number 6879

ISBN 0-310-25740-9

To Chris, Steve, Debbie, and Sharon,
our children,
whose love, encouragement, and support
means so very much to Mrs. Halverson
and me these days

Special Acknowledgment

Very special thanks is due Mrs. Ruth Graves, one of the faithful women of our congregation, who typed the manuscript for this book.

Introduction

The purpose of this devotional book is to help the reader think about his faith and allow it to work out in his life during the week. It is hoped that it will instruct, encourage, and stimulate the reader to see faith in Christ not as a department of life, but as the foundation and fountainhead of life, influencing pervasively all a person is, thinks, and does. This is the biblical way.

The Bible is a Hebrew book, written, except for Luke and Acts, by Jews. The Hebrews conceived of life as unity and wholeness, unlike the Greeks who compartmentalized life. Unfortunately the Greek way of thinking has greatly influenced Western thought about religion in general and the Christian faith in particular. For many, Christianity is something separate from life, involving structures (buildings), forms (worship), practices (prayer, Bible reading, etc.), and language (theological and/or spiritual) which are reserved primarily for a particular time on a particular day in a particular place and which have little if anything to do with one's private, domestic, social, or vocational affairs.

Biblical faith must be understood in a Hebrew context. Man is a unity. Faith is life—life is faith: what one is, feels, thinks, says, does. It is hoped that these devotional readings will help recover this wholeness so characteristic of Jesus Himself ("I do nothing of myself . . . I do only that which pleases the Father."). This is true humanness, man in his perfection, the legacy of the one who will allow the life of God in Christ to work in him by faith.

Furthermore, faith must be nurtured daily. It is not enough to consume one big morsel of biblical truth a week, any more than one could endure for a week on one big Sunday meal. Daily refreshing is essential to the life of faith. God's grace cannot be stored up against future exigencies. Like the manna in the wilderness, it is available as needed in any amount whatever the circumstances. "As your days, so shall your strength be" (Deut. 33:25).

We live life one day at a time, moment by moment, and the secret of a relevant faith for any and all situations is daily exercise in biblical study, meditation, thought, and prayer.

> *Therefore I tell you, do not worry about your life.* —Matthew 6:25

Note from the editor—
These devotional thoughts are divided so they may be used during the workweek, Monday through Friday. At the end you will find two weeks devoted especially to Advent and Lenten thoughts.

Something new under the sun—the new year! You've probably outgrown New Year's resolutions, but you still find yourself taking personal inventory. The temptation to determine that some things are going to be different is irresistible.

For a realistic and promising approach, take a page from the Book of Joshua. The situation is relevant: Israel was preparing for a great adventure—entering and possessing the Promised Land. It had already been given to them, but they had to take it! "Every place that the sole of your foot will tread upon I have given you" (Josh. 1:3). The land was theirs, but they had to stake their claim. So the new year belongs to the man who claims it through faith in the promise of God.

It was a new way: "You have not passed this way before" (Josh. 3:4). Israel had drifted for forty years because of unbelief and disobedience, but now a new way beckoned. The failure of the past would not contaminate the future. That's the way the grace of God works. It covers the past in the gracious and inexhaustible mercy of God. "The blood of Jesus, his Son, purifies us from every sin" (1 John 1:7). In Christ you start with a clean slate, without a record; by His sacrifice you are absolved from all sin and failure.

Because the way was new, Israel needed divine direction, "that you may know the way you shall go" (Josh. 3:4). Joshua 3 gives them the formula for that direction: they were to wait until God moved, then follow. You may enjoy such direction if you are willing to wait on God. You'll never wait too long, never waste any time.

> *Trust in the Lord with all your heart, and do not rely on your own insight. In all your ways acknowledge him, and he will make straight your paths.*
>
> —Proverbs 3:5-6

 Tuesday

Jesus Christ began His public ministry with a fellowship! In the words of Mark, "He appointed twelve . . . that they might be with him (Mark 3: 14). Christ spent most of His time, reserved most of His instruction, for the Twelve. Their fellowship during those three years involved a growing commitment to Christ and a growing commitment to each other. Devotion to Christ was not enough; they had to learn to live together, to love one another, to honor one another, to serve one another, and to work in harmony. Jesus Christ was shaping, molding, fashioning His "first team."

They were to be "sent forth to preach," but they needed to learn the meaning of reconciliation by daily practice, and they needed to learn interdependence. Their proclamation of reconciliation would be empty if their performance did not demonstrate what they preached. Apparently one did not pass the test. He committed himself neither to Christ nor to the others. He was committed exclusively to the purse.

That band of eleven men became the nucleus, the core, of the first Christian community born on Pentecost. And that little community born of the Spirit on Pentecost became the matrix of the mission ·with which Jesus Christ mandated His church. Fellowship is fundamental to mission! Commitment to Christ, commitment to each other in Christ, is prerequisite to authenic Christian witness. Jesus prayed,

> *That all of them may be one, Father,*
> *just as you are in me and I am in you.*
> *May they also be in us so that the world*
> *may believe that you have sent me.*
>
> —John 17:21

 Wednesday

A church preoccupied with itself. What a pity!

Pastor, officers, and people filled with concern for their own welfare: their buildings, their comfort, their programs. Emphasis on "getting more members." Struggling to keep members busy with the establishment, increase attendance at meetings, build (and boast) a large congregation. Everything that competes for interest and involvement of members is treated as a threat, feared and often criticized.

What a caricature of authentic Christianity! What a contrast with a Lord whose life was given away in love for others! Its very concern for itself is blocking fulfillment. Its inwardness is self-defeating. Turned in on itself, it can get nowhere, obviously, except further in!

And all the while the world outside languishes for the love of Christ, the compassion and understanding and acceptance which Christ alone can give. The extrovert God of John 3:16 ("For God so loved the world that he gave his one and only Son") does not beget an introvert people. The God who loves us even when we are rebels ("But God demonstrates his own love for us in this: While we were still sinners, Christ died for us" Rom. 5:8.) is not honored by a nonaccepting people insulated against and isolated from the world for which Christ died! The world waits, and responds, when it sees a demonstration of the unconditional love of God in those who profess to be followers of God. And the church which so demonstrates will grow up and out, not in and down! Jesus' word to His disciples applies to them collectively as well as individually:

> *For whoever wants to save his life will lose it, but whoever loses his life for me and for the gospel will save it.*
> —Mark 8:35

 Thursday

"Destination sickness"—the syndrome of the man who has arrived and discovered he is nowhere! He has achieved his goals and finds they are not what he had anticipated. He suffers the disillusionment of promises that petered out—the pay-off with the kickback! He has all the things money can buy and finds decreasing satisfaction in all that he has. He is satiated and unsatisfied! He's got a pot full of nothing! He's in the land of ulcers and cardiacs, alcoholism, divorce, and suicide! He suffers from the "neurosis of emptiness." He's the man who has become a whale of a success downtown and a pathetic failure at home. He's a big shot with the boys in the office and a big phony with the boys at home. He's a status symbol in society and a fake with the family. "Destination sickness"—the illness peculiar to a culture that is affluent—and godless!

The cure is Jesus Christ. He is available anytime, anywhere to any man! He said,

> *Here I am! I stand at the door and knock. If anyone hears my voice and opens the door, I will go in and eat with him.*
>
> —Revelation 3:20

> *For in Christ all the fullness of the Deity lives in bodily form, and you have this fullness in Christ.* —Colossians 2:9-10

> *Blessed are those who hunger and thirst for righteousness, for they will be filled.*
>
> —Matthew 5:6

 Friday

Have you ever let yourself be prejudiced against a man before you knew him? Ever allowed criticism to predispose you so that your mind was made up about the man before you were introduced? When you finally meet him, you're unable to accept him at face value because prejudgment has distorted your thinking. You find yourself resisting the man; he's "behind the eight ball" right from the start. Then you begin to get acquainted, warm up to him, discover you have misjudged, and feel ashamed for swallowing the criticism so readily.

Men do this with Jesus Christ! They let misrepresentation prejudice them, predispose them against Him before they get to know Christ Himself. Sometimes an overzealous, well-meaning Christian oversells, giving the impression he's trying to force his beliefs on a man. The man digs in, refuses to budge—but in rejecting the dogma, he rejects Christ the Person. Instead of letting Christ speak for Himself, instead of taking Him at face value, the person may close his mind. (Note: Some Christians condemn Jesus Christ to rejection because they are so busy trying to win men to their point of view rather than to Christ Himself.) Sometimes a Christian fails to be all he should be, and we allow this failure to reflect against Jesus Christ.

Give Jesus Christ the courtesy of His own defense! Get acquainted with Him. You'll discover He is quite different than sometimes made to appear by an indiscreet disciple. In the first four books of the New Testament you have four brief eyewitness accounts of this most fascinating life ever lived. You'll be amazed and thrilled when you meet the central Figure about whom these records speak, for He makes Himself known through them. Familiarize yourself with the record before allowing yourself to be prejudiced. Make up your own mind on the basis of the facts. Give yourself the benefit of a firsthand faith, a firsthand experience of Christ Himself! After all, this is authentic Christianity: A personal relationship with Christ.

A Christian is one who knows Christ and has accepted Him. The relationship is intensely personal and eternal! Until you know Jesus Christ this way, you're missing the best things in life. In fact, you're missing life itself. For to know Him is to have life everlasting.

> *Now this is eternal life: that men may know you, the only true God, and Jesus Christ, whom you have sent.* —John 17:3

 Monday

Many of us pray the prayer once a week, and if God answers prayer (which He does), the evil consequences are incalculable: "Forgive us our trespasses as we forgive those who trespass against us." That's the prayer, part of the so-called "Lord's Prayer" which many of us pray as we worship each Sunday.

If God answers that prayer, what incredible judgment upon some—for they simply refuse to forgive those who trespass against them! It is no wonder the church has lost its power. No wonder faith is unreal. No wonder the large majority of

14

Americans (according to a recent poll) consider the Christian religion irrelevant. If God forgives as we forgive, and that is what we are asking Him to do when we pray that prayer, how many of us live in broken relationship with God?

When Jesus taught the "Lord's Prayer," He lifted from it that one petition as if to say, "This is crucial." He said quite plainly, "If you do not forgive men their sins, your Father will not forgive your sins" (Matt. 6:15). In other words, you can't be right with God if you're not right with others. Which was the point of His instruction: "If you are offering your gift at the altar and there remember that your brother has something against you, leave your gift there.... First go and be reconciled to your brother; then come and offer your gift" (Matt. 5:23-24).

Reconciliation demands priority! Undoubtedly the explanation for much of the deadness in Christian experience is our refusal to be reconciled. There is nothing important until you have done that!

Forgive, and you will be forgiven.
—Luke 6:37

 Tuesday

Exercise in futility: the struggle to produce a

kingdom of God society without kingdom of God men. This is the deepest frustration in history! Frustration, ironically, which every generation seems to suffer, despite the lesson of history. It has its roots in man's pride, his passion to believe in man, his stubborn refusal to accept sin as endemic in human nature, his insistence on the perfectability of man by education, organization, and legislation.

You see this frustration preeminently in youth today as their idealism gets smashed again and again, leaving them confused and angry. They mistrust their parents and the institutions their parents have built. They believe in themselves, their ideals, their possibilities. Then they see so much in their own generation which contradicts their belief; they see intransigence in their elders and, without realizing it, they yield to despair. Futility mocks their brave dream.

"Essential humanism is man's rebellion against and alienation from God. This is man's slavery. How can that which produced man's slavery set him free from it? All man's efforts to possess a self-contained freedom, to find the meaning of life by his own wisdom, to build a worthy human society without God, are self-defeating, for they are a denial of man's essential nature."[*]

You can't have a kingdom of God society without kingdom of God men! If it were possible,

[*]Donald G. Miller, president of Pittsburgh Seminary, in *Christianity Today*, May 8, 1970.

men like Nicodemus could have managed it; and Jesus said to Nicodemus: "You must be born again" (John 3:7). The issue is unequivocal—

Unless a man is born again, he cannot see the kingdom of God.   —John 3:3

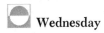 **Wednesday**

Speaking over the NBC network some time ago, Dr. Maurice N. Eisendrath, president of the Union of American Hebrew Congregations, said, "If I were a Christian minister instead of a Jewish teacher, there is nothing I would lament so much, and bitterly resent, as this wholesale transformation by myriads of 'Christians' and by some Jews of what should be, in its deeper meaning, a solemn and sacred day set apart to recall the birth of him whom I, if I were a Christian, would call my Savior. To almost every Christian it does seem strange and inexplicable that the appealing, alluring, ennobling Jew of Nazareth should be rejected by anyone sensitive to the nobler prompting of the human spirit or of the divine image within the human soul. But did the Jews really reject Jesus? Of course they did not. Why, as a matter of fact, the only ones who actually accepted him during his brief sojourn on earth were Jews.

"So to me as a rabbi, the most important question before us in this generation is not whether or why the Jews supposedly rejected Jesus, but whether the multitudes of 'Christians' have genuinely accepted him. I fear for the most part they have not. For if they had, it would seem to me there would be in our world today neither poverty nor greed, neither hatred nor bigotry, neither wars nor preparation for wars; but there would be instead only peace on earth to men of good will everywhere." (The rabbi went on to imagine Jesus returning to earth, entering the houses of worship bearing His name, finding anti-Semitism and other forms of bigotry there. He continued.)

"To honor Christ as God incarnate and then to sneer at the people from whom he sprang is strangely inconsistent and despicable as well. It is sufficient to incur the wrath of God and bring down his punishment upon us. As Jesus would wander from house to house, he would note on the one hand Christmas trees bent low with gifts so lavish they would provide sustenance for many a family for many a year. The conviction would grow upon him that this generation is more selfish, greedy, and sinful than the one which sent him to the cross. No, it is not just the Jews who do not accept Jesus—it is the vast majority of our generation!"

He who is not with me is against me.
—Matthew 12:30

If anyone is ashamed of me and my words, the Son of Man will be ashamed of him when he comes in his glory.
—Luke 9:26

 Thursday

"Religion and politics don't mix!" So leave politics to the irreligious and don't complain when government goes godless! "Business and religion don't mix." So leave business to the ungodly and don't be surprised when business goes totally secular. Why should we expect politicians to legislate, adjudicate, and govern with spiritual and moral insights if we insist on keeping God out of government? Why should business practices conform to biblical ethics if we separate faith from the marketplace?

But both are a denial of the soul of Christian faith: Incarnation! In Jesus Christ God involved Himself in man's affairs, in his politics, business, society, in the whole warp and woof of human activity. Religion that separates itself from the world is a cop out! It is not the religion of Jesus Christ who was concerned for the whole man in the totality of his being. The true disciple of Christ will reflect His concern, His love, His influence, His involvement in the total human situation. "Your attitude should be the same as that of Christ Jesus: Who, being in very nature God, did not consider equality with God something to be grasped, but made himself nothing, taking the very nature of a servant, being made in human likeness. And being found in appearance as a man, he humbled himself and became obedient to death—even death on a cross!" (Phil. 3:5-8).

> *He that is greatest in the kingdom of God is everybody's servant.*
> —Jesus (paraphrase)

 Friday

Self-interest is deadly! If it becomes primary in a man's thinking. Self-centeredness is characteristic of insanity; it is impossible for the mentally ill person to see life from any but his own point of view. You can't reason with him; there's no point of contact because his total frame of reference is self. Of course this is the ultimate in self-centeredness, but the fact is that most of us narrow down our lives too much in this respect. Efficiency, productivity, and satisfaction are greatly diminished in the self-centered man. Life becomes increasingly ingrown because whatever is at the center of life is its circumference! When self is central, energies of body, mind, and heart are turned in on self. Life becomes small, confined, tight, inflexible.

Diagram life as a spiral and you get the picture: a self-centered life is a spiral turning inward, tighter and tighter until it reaches dead center. There's no place to go! Life halts—snags at the impasse. "Give me" is its slogan. What begins as a desire for self-realization actually ends up as the opposite—complete frustration. The pay-off is futility! Unself-centeredness is like a spiral beginning at the center and turning outward. There is no limit; it unwinds, out and out, wider and wider, ad-infinitum. The slogan of this life is "use me!" This really describes love. Man is much like a hole: the more you take away from him the bigger he gets. Greatness is always in terms of giving, not getting. Black absorbs all light—hence darkness; white reflects light.

The ultimate in unself-centeredness is to be Christ-centered! God at the center of your life—God the circumference also. Seeing life God's way. Evaluating life in terms of eternity.

Who is at the center of your life? Why do you work so hard? What drives you, keeps you so everlastingly at it? Is it all for self, or for Christ and eternity? The most strategic thing one can do is center his life outside himself in the living Christ. Quit thinking, worrying, and fussing about self. Give yourself away to God daily. Live for Him!

> *For whoever wants to save his life will lose it, but whoever loses his life for me ...will save it.* —Mark 8:35

 Monday

Servant! Synonymous with greatness in the kingdom of God. Personified in Jesus Christ. He was the servant incarnate, to be emulated by His followers. Jesus did not just serve men; He was their servant! There's a difference. Some serve condescendingly, patronizingly—as though the recipients of their service are second-class citizens. And far too often they demand recognition (if nothing more) for their service, which indicates service not for the sake of serving, but for the sake of self.

Not so the servant. When he has done his best, he has done what he should. His satisfaction is not a reward, but the delight in pleasing his master. The servant of God lives for others. His love for God is expressed in his love for man. He serves God by serving his neighbor. And all men are his neighbors—even his enemies!

But is this not expecting too much from a man?

It is! Which is precisely why Jesus Christ is taken seriously by so few. Who can argue that the greatest single need in our time is the gracious neighbor serving others in the love of Jesus Christ?

Whoever wants to become great among you must be your servant, and whoever wants to be first must be slave of all.
—Mark 10:43-44

 Tuesday

What is a Christian? The word is ambiguous, even in a "Christian" culture. A "Christian" in the Western world may be anyone who is not a Jew or a Hindu or a Moslem or a Buddhist, etc. To some it means anyone who is "civilized," whatever that means.

There are many kinds of "Christians": Catholic, Protestant, Anglican, Methodist, Baptist, Lutheran, Presbyterian, etc. Some are "conservative," some "liberal," some "moderate," some "radical," and some "reactionary." Some are pacifists, some militarists. Imagine the confusion in a non-Christian land where "Christians" compete for converts or criticize and condemn one another. Nobody is ever sure what is meant by "Christian" unless the one who uses the word is careful to define his terms.

This ambiguity is not true of Jesus Christ! Men may disagree with what He said, or they may deny that He said it by discrediting the record. But they all know what is meant when one speaks of Jesus Christ. With few exceptions, there is a universal respect for Christ, even among those who hold other religious views. He provides a common ground upon which men may communicate. The point is, we ought to be speaking more about Jesus Christ and less about Christianity. Jesus Christ is the issue! Not the church, not our views about Him, but Christ Himself!

> *For God so loved the world that he gave his one and only Son, that whoever believes in him shall not perish but have everlasting life.* —John 3:16

 Wednesday

Evangelism is not salesmanship! It is not urging people, pressing them, coercing them, overwhelming them, or subduing them. Evangelism is telling a message. Evangelism is reporting good news. Evangelism is witnessing to certain objective his-

24

torical facts and their relevancy in one's personal experience. Evangelism is speaking with the authority of Jesus Christ in the power and love of God the Holy Spirit. Evangelism does not resort to canned speeches or sales gimmicks for its effectiveness, nor does it rely on Madison Avenue pitches.

In fact, rightly understood, evangelism is not the work of man at all; it is the work of the Holy Spirit. He entered history for this purpose; He indwelt the church at Pentecost in order to do His evangelistic work through her. He will perform His evangelistic task in and through any man who will yield to His infilling and submit to His control. This does not mean that legitimate methods are to be abandoned, nor that the Christian can ignore training and study and personal application. But it does mean that He does not depend upon any of these in and of themselves for effectiveness. It does mean He wants the best of methods and discipline and application made servants of the Holy Spirit.

Evangelism is not just a department of the church to which a few are to be devoted while others busy themselves with things equally important. Evangelism is the work of the whole church, her raison d'etre. By it the church is meant to invade the world for the kingdom of Christ, infect the world with the kingdom's ethos. Every benefit the church has to offer the world emerges from her evangelistic mission, and to the extent that she is faithful to this mission, she blesses the world.

> *When he (the Spirit) comes, he will prove the world wrong about sin and righteousness and judgment. . . . he will guide you into all truth. . . . He will bring glory to me.* —John 16:8, 13-14

Thursday

"The church must leave its buildings and be prepared really to live among the people." Quoting the above, a writer responded, "Today with all its great opportunities and challenges open to the church, one has to admit that it is exactly what the observer misses, to see the church in action and in the midst of the problems eagerly searching for solutions." Now this is a familiar—familiar? monotonous! criticism of the church today. No doubt it richly deserves much of it.

But what is it that this "observer" (whoever he is) misses? What is he looking for? How will he know when the church is "in action, in the midst of the problem"? And where is the church if she does not "really live among the people"? She is certainly in her buildings only a few hours a week at the most. How is she supposed to identify herself when she leaves her buildings and lives among the people? Should the church carry banners? Or wear buttons or badges? Perhaps all Christians should adopt a uniform to help this mythical "observer" in his distress. For that matter, who's been doing all the good in the world? Apparently Christians have not. Apparently, whoever is doing it, the church is not! Is all the good being done by atheists? By non-church people? Or what is meant by the church? The clergy? The executives? The board secretaries?

If by the church we mean the members, they are living among the people most of the time, in the homes and marketplaces, the offices and schools, the farms and factories. The church is everywhere! And quietly, faithfully, anonymously she is at work, influencing benevolently, by a multitude of means, the social structures around her. She is, to be specific, the "salt of the earth." True, she has lost her savor at times, but just because one cannot see her does not mean she is not there. In fact, as long as salt retains its identity, it is useless. It must penetrate to benefit, and when it does, it disappears! Salt is doing its work only when it is invisible. So is the church! She'll never get the credit for what she does any more than her Lord did. He was perfect, and they crucified Him!

You are the salt of the earth.
—Matthew 5:13

Friday

One does not become Christian simply by embracing Christian ethics! Christian ethics are the fruit of vital faith in Jesus Christ. Society will never be made Christian by imposing upon it certain ethical standards. You don't Christianize collective man by legislating righteousness! Christian influence within society is the product of the individual Christian in that society. We should not be surprised when society does not think and act Christian. We should not be shocked when government does not think and act Christian.

There is no such thing as a Christian government, unless you refer to the kingdom of our Lord and Savior Jesus Christ. There is no such thing as a Christian society, unless you refer to the society of the redeemed, the community of those who have been regenerated through the power of the Gospel of Jesus Christ. Western civilization is Christian in a general sort of way of course. But our present Christian culture is not firsthand; it is residual. For the most part we are living off the capital (the interest has long since been depleted) of a Christian dedication and morality produced by the Reformation, the Wesleyan revival, and other local revivals.

Where Christ rules, there only is Christian government. The only Christian society is the true church of Jesus Christ, composed of all those everywhere who have received Christ as Savior and Lord, who have been redeemed by His precious blood. Inevitably the world is a better place because of the society of the redeemed, and conversely the whole world suffers where the church is not or where the church becomes something less than the church. Like salt, authentic Christianity purifies and preserves the society it penetrates. As the level of Christian dedication rises, the level of the society in which those Christians dwell rises. What we need today is not more legislation to produce a moral, ethical, righteous nation; what we need is for the church to be the church, for Christians to be Christian in fact. The church of Jesus Christ is the key to national strength, the clue to national decay.

> *Righteousness exalts a nation, but sin is a reproach to any people.*
> —Proverbs 14:34

 Monday

What is the greatest frontier for America? It is not a geographical frontier, nor political, economical, military, educational, nor scientific and technological—it is not space. It is a *spiritual* frontier!

29

This is the greatest frontier that has ever challenged a generation of Americans, and it supersedes all other frontiers. Because if this frontier is not conquered, all other frontiers are lost. This is inevitable!

At the close of the war with Japan, General MacArthur said, "This is no longer a military problem, nor an economic, nor a political problem —it is a theological problem. If we are to save the flesh—we must save the spirit." The situation has not changed, except to become more acute! A genuine spiritual awakening is the only legitimate hope for the future. It must be more than a mere revival of religious interest. We have had that: church and church school attendance breaking all records, religious books and periodicals hitting the best seller lists with monotonous regularity, religious songs not uncommonly at the top of popularity polls. But at the same time there has been an alarming increase in crime: juvenile delinquency, divorce, drug addiction, alcoholism. Will Herberg, the highly respected Jewish theologian, points out in his book, *Protestant, Catholic, Jew*, that "at the same time she is becoming more religious—America is becoming more secular." The only thing that will conquer this spiritual frontier, without which all other frontiers are lost, is a revival of righteousness and honesty and godly living.

This spiritual frontier demands the *highest heroism!* It demands pioneers: pioneers with all the strength, courage, endurance, and determination of those brave men and women who conquered the geographical frontiers of a century ago. It demands sacrifice: the kind of a sacrifice a man pays when he refuses to go along with a godless crowd laughing at lewd jokes and mocking purity and moderation. It demands risk: the risk of being "dropped" by the gang or ridiculed with the label of piousness or mid-Victorianism. It demands men—brave men—men of God. Men who will stand against the tide of brazen, loud-mouthed, leering drunkenness and immorality that foreshadow the doom of any people or nation. Men who are convinced that America can never be defeated from without unless she is first weakened within—that no force is great enough to conquer a country that is strong with righteousness—that the nation spiritually strong is invulnerable!

> *Righteousness exalts a nation, but sin is a reproach to any people.*
> —Proverbs 14:34

 Tuesday

How is the Gospel relevant?
How is love relevant to loneliness, forgiveness

relevant to guilt? How is purity relevant to evil, hope relevant to despair? How is light relevant to darkness, cleanness relevant to filth? How is peace relevant to confusion, order relevant to disorder? How is water relevant to thirst, food relevant to hunger? How is fulfillment relevant to futility, realization relevant to frustration? How is reality relevant to illusion, truth relevant to error? How is purpose relevant to meaninglessness, fulness relevant to emptiness? How is victory relevant to defeat, achievement relevant to failure? How is life relevant to death, resurrection relevant to the grave?

What love is to loneliness, forgiveness is to guilt, purity is to evil, hope is to despair, light is to darkness, cleanness is to filth, peace is to confusion, order is to disorder, water is to thirst, food is to hunger, fulfillment is to futility, realization is to frustration, reality is to illusion, truth is to error, purpose is to meaninglessness, fullness is to emptiness, victory is to defeat, and achievement is to failure. What life is to death, resurrection is to the grave—that is how the Gospel is relevant!

In their lust for relevance men have emasculated the Gospel, making it hopelessly irrelevant. They have made it the servant of their human systems: capitalism or socialism, militarism or pacifism, segregation or integration, conservatism or liberalism, progressivism or the status quo, etc. Men do not make the Gospel relevant! What impertinence. What presumption. The Gospel is "the power of

God." Men do not manage the power of God; they serve it! It is the timelessness of the Gospel which makes it relevant today as it was nineteen centuries ago, as it was 2,000 years before Christ in Abraham's day (Rom. 4). The changeless Gospel is eternally contemporary, perennially practical, addressing itself to all human need in every generation, every century, every millennium.

Therefore, let us preach it! Let us proclaim it! Let us herald it! Let us be its witnesses! Let us not rest until all the world has heard!

Go into all the world. —Mark 16:15

 Wednesday

There are those who are so "heavenly minded they're no earthly good"! Their religion is utterly unlike that of the Lord they profess. The holiness of Jesus worked in actual life. He did not run from the secular; He was immersed in it! His holiness was not for the ivory tower or the sequestered existence; it was for life! It was not for the monastery; it was for the road! The Pharisees couldn't figure Him. He was a mystery to them. He was continually breaking their religious rules. Jesus was inconsistent to the religionists of His day, but He was thoroughly consistent with His Father in heaven. Religion to Jesus was not rules but *love:*

love for God and love for the needy, the dispossessed, the sick, the sinful, the unholy.

Jesus accused the religionists of emptying God's Word of its meaning by "teaching for doctrines the commandments of men." (It's easier to obey rules than to love men.) Pseudo holiness can't take the wear and tear of daily life. It tries to escape actualities with rules and regulations which help to vindicate its escapism. In the name of what is miscalled "separation" some isolate themselves from the world and insulate themselves against its sin, leaving an impassable gulf between them and the very people they ought to be loving and helping. Hence the secular man doesn't take Christians seriously! He hasn't seen demonstrated a faith that has everyday answers. He is unimpressed with Christians because their faith seems so irrelevant.

The Pharisees called Jesus a "drunkard, winebibber, glutton." To them He was irreligious, secular, blasphemous. And Jesus would come in for the identical criticism today by some who have managed to lose contact completely with the world God loves and for whom Christ died!

"You are the salt of the earth." Salt works on contact; otherwise it is useless. "You are the light of the world." Light was meant to penetrate darkness, not flee from it. A Christian can escape certain tensions in the conflict between good and evil by running away from the world's burdens, but to do so is to repudiate the authentic Christian way. Love takes the initiative! Love is self-less! Love is not preoccupied with its own white-ness, but with the needy.

> *You are the salt of the earth.... You*
> *are the light of the world.*
> —Matthew 5:13-14

 Thursday

What is the range of Christian responsibility? Where are its borders? Assuming the Christian's obligation to his own family and work, what is his responsibility beyond these?

Is it limited to evangelism? Take the conventional view of evangelism: to preach (or witness) the Gospel in order to convert men to Christ and nurture them in their new-found faith. Is that the limit of Christian responsibility? Does the Christian bear no burden for his community beyond evangelism? Do the actions of school boards and teachers, police and firemen, politicians and public officials have no concern for him? Are poverty, war, and social disorder outside his citizenship?

Is it conceivable that beyond his own family and work and church organization the Christian has no responsibility except evangelism? If so, then whose responsibility are these great public and community problems? How does the Christian exercise and manifest his faith in the midst of his community if it is not directed toward resolution and improvement? Who is to inform public officials and bring pressure to bear upon their decisions if not the Christian? What does he mean by his Sunday prayer, "Thy will be done on earth as it is in heaven," if he is indifferent to the conditions of the society of which he is a part? Does he expect the decisions to be made, the actions to be taken, the work to be done, the movements to be generated by the non-Christian? If this is the way he thinks, why is he surprised by decisions and actions and work and movements that do not conform to his Christian principles? Jesus said to His disciples,

You are the salt of the earth.
—Matthew 5:13

 Friday

Is it conceivable that a man is really interested in the kingdom of God in the future if he is indifferent to social conditions here and now? Can he be giving priority to "the kingdom of God

and its righteousness" as his Lord commanded if he is not doing all in his power to translate that priority into reality where he is in all that he is doing?

Faith, in the biblical sense, is not intellectual assent to dogma. Faith is commitment to a Person which issues in obedience and action! Faith in the biblical sense produces change—change in the one who believes and who in turn begins to change his environment. Which is why authentic spiritual awakening has always resulted in social revolution, as, for example, the radical reforms born out of the Wesleyan revival in England, affecting child labor, slavery, general working conditions, the common man, and the church.

The key to such revolution is not ecclesiastical authority or size or wealth or status. The key to such revolution is the power of God! Which is released when men acknowledge the ugly disparity between their profession and their practice and when they confess their sins and desire the will of God in their lives and in their situations. In other words, when men repent!

The need is not for more education or more legislation or more organization. The need is for repentance!

If my people who are called by my name humble themselves, and pray and seek my face, and turn from their wicked ways, then I will hear from heaven, and

will forgive their sin and heal their land.
—2 Chronicles 7:14

 Monday

Non-involvement is the antithesis of authentic Christianity! Christian faith began with a man who was so involved with humanity, with its aches and pains and diseases, with its tragedy and hunger and alienation, that He was an enigma to His contemporaries and a bother to the religionists who took pains to parade their piety. When everything else failed, they saw to His crucifixion.

He made religion relevant! He identified with man at the point of his deepest needs. He involved Himself with man at his worst. In the words of one apostle, "He became sin for us." That's the "last full measure of devotion." That's love at its best!

That is what Christianity is all about. The Bible is the record of a God who cared—cared enough to go as far as necessary to help men, even when they were in revolt against Him, even when man didn't care for God.

Christ did not come for the unsoiled, respectable, pious pretenders. He came for the unwashed, the sinful, the lost. To do this He turned his back on divine prerogative, "made himself of no reputation," "humbled himself," "became obedient unto death—even the death of the cross." He traded His glory for man's sin that man might share His glory! He repudiated His riches for man's poverty that man might enjoy His riches! He suffered man's penalty for sin that man might be infused with His eternal life! The Christian who is following his Lord will be identified and involved with human need at its deepest levels. That is simply indisputable!

> *Have this mind among yourselves, which is yours in Christ Jesus, who, though he was in the form of God, did not count equality with God a thing to be grasped, but emptied himself, taking the form of a servant, being born in the likeness of men.* —Philippians 2:5-7

 Tuesday

There was a time when man was one. No language barrier—no racial issue. "And Cain said to Abel his brother, 'Let us go out to the field.' And when they were in the field, Cain rose up against his brother Abel and killed him" (Gen. 4:8). "Lamech said to his wives, 'Adah and Zillah, hear my voice; you wives of Lamech, hearken to what I say: I have slain a man for wounding me'" (Gen. 4:23).

No language barrier—no racial issue, but there was violence!

There was a time when man was one. No language barrier—no racial issue. "The Lord saw that the wickedness of man was great in the earth, and that every imagination of the thoughts of his heart was only evil continually. And the Lord was sorry that he had made man on the earth, and it grieved him to his heart. So the Lord said, 'I will blot out man whom I have created from the face of the ground'" (Gen. 6:5-7).

No language barrier—no racial issue, but there was universal immorality!

There was a time when man was one. "Now the whole earth had one language. . . . And they said to one another, 'Come, let us build ourselves a city, and a tower with its top in the heavens, and let us make a name for ourselves, lest we be scattered abroad upon the face of the whole earth.'. . . And the Lord said, 'Behold, they are one people, and they have all one language; and this is only the beginning of what they will do; and nothing that they propose to do will now be impossible for them. Come, let us go down, and there confuse their language, that they may not understand one another's speech.' So the Lord scattered them abroad from there over the face of the all the earth" (Gen. 11:1, 4, 6-8).

The problem is deeper than race or language! Elimination of racial and language issues will not eliminate immorality, crime, violence, or war. Things aren't really very different in our modern nuclear space-age world than they were in the world pictured in the first eleven chapters of Genesis. More sophisticated perhaps, but not different. Whatever it was that made Cain kill his brother—made the imaginations of men's hearts only evil continually—caused men to aspire to a city, a tower reaching to heaven, a name—whatever it was, God found it necessary to confound human language, to fragment humanity. And ever since man has been trying to make alliances which leave God out!

The Bible is the record of God's remedy for history's futility: God's redemptive work in the person of His Son, Jesus Christ.

> *So God created man in his own image, in the image of God he created him; male and female he created them.*
> —Genesis 1:27

 **Wednesday**

It is not our differences that are the problem— it is our indifference! Diversity is of the essence of life. Without diversity there would be no design. The tapestry would have no beauty apart from the various colored threads woven into its exquisite pattern. The painting would portray nothing without differences in shade and hue. The novel would be unreal without conflicting characters.

Life is diverse, whether it is the flowers or the trees or the animals or the fowls or the fish or the insects. This is one of the strengths of man: his diversity, his ability to fulfill a role someone else is unable to fulfill—to be a team. Thank God for differences!

But indifference? Who can abide it? It is the enemy of man, the enemy of society. It is abdication from life! Twentieth century America suffers incalculably from this disease.

Think what would happen if every person accepted his role, however high or low his station, and lived it. If every affluent family did something for one needy family. If every white person took responsibility to relate to one black person. If every man thought of himself as a committee of one to bring reconciliation and resolution to the social ills that are so deeply dividing our nation at this time.

You can't do everything for everybody. You can do something for someone.

As a prisoner for the Lord, then, I urge you to live a life worthy of the calling you have received. —Ephesians 4:1

What kind of testimony do you have? Are you a witness of what God has done for you in Christ or a witness of what you have been able to do for yourself? Are you a demonstration of self-sufficiency or a testimony to the adequacy of the grace of God in Christ? When unbelievers look at you, are they impressed simply with a man who has managed to live a relatively good life or is there something about you that testifies to the reality and relevancy of Christ in your life?

At this point much so-called Christian testimony breaks down. Reduced to simplest terms, apart from the window dressing of pious language, many testimonies are nothing more than personal success stories. One man was able to break a bothersome habit, another spends thirty minutes a day in prayer, or reads through the Bible in a year, or memorizes so many verses of Scripture, etc. Still another tells how cleverly he answered a skeptic and "put him in his place." The side of their lives they talk about is that which shows what they are doing and how well they are handling themselves or others. Such testimonies put the accent on the man's moral, ethical, and/or religious achievements. Absent from them is the authentic note of the Christian witness.

They do not glorify God! They do not bring conviction to the hearer, nor manifest the love of Christ to the unbeliever, nor help him understand the Gospel of God's love in the sacrifice and resurrection of His Son. In fact, they perpetuate the delusion that being a Christian is just a matter of living a good life and maybe following some religious practices.

Not that the good life is not important. Not that prayer and Bible reading and Scripture memorization are to be disregarded. But they are the fruit of a life that has been redeemed by Christ, forgiven and cleansed by His "precious blood." Good works speak for themselves, and if they don't, we might as well be silent.

> *Let your light shine before men, that they may see your good deeds and praise your Father in heaven.* —Matthew 5:16

 Friday

Revolution is not radical! Revolution is reactionary—as reactionary as repression. They are alternate strokes of the same cycle driving from one extreme to the other. Both are wrong. Both perpetuate the evil they profess to resolve. Both generate hostility, violence, and alienation. Both are idolatrous because they are essentially vindictive, and vengeance is the prerogative of God!

Neither is constructive. They trigger each other's destructive reaction. One is set blindly to preserve the status quo, while the other is determined to destroy the status quo. Both are preoccupied with the status quo and have no positive designs for change.

Forgiveness is radical! Forgiveness halts the vicious reactionary cycle of revolution and repression and sets a course for constructive change. Forgiveness dissolves alienation, brings reconciliation, restoration, and renewal. Forgiveness is the most radical force in history. Jesus is the most radical person in history.

> *But God demonstrates his own love for us in this: While we were still sinners (rebels), Christ died for us.*
> —Romans 5:8

 Monday

The logic of the Gospel confronts our day with irresistible force. Five inexorable arguments demand the necessity of exploiting every resource to propagate the Gospel:

(1) The Great Commission leaves no room for debate. Jesus commanded the church to "teach

all nations," and her only alternative is to disobey. If there were no other justification for missions, this command alone would make neglect unpardonable.

(2) The Apostle Paul declared that Christ's love constrains us with the convincing argument that "we are convinced that one died for all, and therefore all died. And he died for all that those who live should no longer live for themselves, but for him who died for them and was raised again" (2 Cor. 5:14-15). What a terrible malady infects the Christian who can remain unmoved and complacent in the face of Christless millions and compounded human tragedy? What coldness, what hardness, what selfishness quenches the love of Christ in a missionless Christian?

(3) History is with Jesus Christ! All the explosive passion of mankind for peace, freedom, justice, and unity will find its fulfillment in Jesus Christ. It is not inconceivable that these days of transition are truly eschatological, that this era of revolution is preface to the most radical transition in history—the end of the age, Christ's Second Advent! Such a hope is powerful incentive for an unprecedented thrust with the Gospel.

(4) Our Lord made it plain that one condition was immediately to precede His return: "And this gospel of the kingdom will be preached in the whole world as a testimony to all nations, and then the end will come" (Matt. 24:14). The possibility of hastening the return of our Lord to con-

summate His redemptive purpose is strong inducement.

(5) Finally, it is more apparent than ever that human nature in and of itself is hopelessly deadlocked. In an era of incomparable progress, when he knows more than he's ever known, man seems less capable than ever of solving his compounding problems. The Gospel of Jesus Christ is the "power of God for salvation." Why should Christians defect to lesser enterprise at a time when man's need for the Gospel is so indisputably demonstrated?

I am not ashamed of the gospel, because it is the power of God for the salvation of everyone who believes. —Romans 1:16

 Tuesday

Unconscious influence is what counts in the long run. It's a man's real influence. Not what he says when he carefully chooses his words, not what he does consciously to impress, not what he is when he's working to make a point, when he has himself under control, but what he is when he's not trying, when he's relaxed. Just the man himself, apart from any effort, the real self keeps coming through to people all the time—comes through what he says, what he does, what he tries to be. And this unconscious influence either confirms or contradicts the impression he is trying to make.

It boils down to this: A man cannot control his real influence! It flows from within him, from deep down underneath his consciousness. Like an iceberg, six-sevenths of a man is below the surface, and this uncontrollable six-sevenths asserts itself constantly. Many a lad has been scarred for life by an influence in his father of which the father was totally unaware. The boy's character was molded, his destiny jelled, in terms of an example in the father over which the father had no control.

For this reason, too, Christ has the solid, practical answer! Because He goes to work at the center of a man's being where it really matters. Jesus told His disciples that it was to their advantage that He return to His Heavenly Father following the resurrection. "It is for your good that I am going away. Unless I go away, the Counselor (the Holy Spirit) will not come to you; but if I go, I will send him to you" (John 16:7). God, by His Spirit, actually indwells the Christian. Working from within, He produces bona fide Christian character, making a man's unconscious influence a Christ-like influence.

True Christianity is not trying to be something a man cannot be. It is literally letting Christ, by the Spirit, be Himself in the Christian's heart. The

Christian, recognizing his own inadequacy, turns the controls of his life over to Christ. Christ, reigning from within, controls the uncontrollable!

Quit trying to be what you can't. Admit your need; submit to Christ.

> *If a man remains in me and I in him, he will bear much fruit; apart from me you can do nothing.* —John 15:5

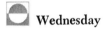 **Wednesday**

The big question in human relations is man's willingness. The issue is volitional, not emotional. The deepest problem in history, and it's universal, is man's will, man's wrong will toward God and man. We blame our emotions, but our hang-ups are a matter of choice, not feeling. Feelings are involved, but they are not critical. The child is mastered by his emotions; the mature person lives by his will. To illustrate, the bed never feels better than when the alarm goes off. Emotionally, staying in bed is desirable, but the responsible person yields to his will and rises.

Take the man who says love for his wife has died; he now loves another woman. "I can't help it," he says, "that's just the way it is," and he sees no way out but divorce. First question is, "Did you mean it when you took your marriage vows?" "Of course I meant it," he says. By what right then does he renege on his unconditional promise? His answer: he's fallen in love with another woman. Which is emotion talking. Which he strongly denies. Very well, let's make the acid test. Is he willing to reconcile with his wife, willing to have his love for her restored? Is he willing to let the other woman go? God is able to restore that marriage better than new. The big question is, "Will he let God do it?"

So it is with a man's relation to God. Will he allow Christ to make Himself real to him; is he willing to try Christ? When the issue's drawn, man begins to fall back on his lame excuses: "You can't prove God. You can't prove the Bible." He's shadowboxing! The fact is, if he is willing, God will! Jesus said,

> *If any man's will is to do his will, he shall know.* —John 7:17 (RSV)

 Thursday

One element of the so-called generation gap is the rediscovery of humanity by the younger generation. Simple human values have come to mean more to them than some of the material values on which their elders have placed so much emphasis and trust. The refusal of youth to accept carte blanche the value system of their parents is disconcerting, to say the least, to a generation which went through two world wars and a never-to-be-forgotten Depression. Their preoccupation during the years the "war babies" have been growing up has been national defense and the gross national product. Which is understandable. But with this has come mushrooming materialism which has failed to bring happiness.

Many modern youth grew up in homes where they had everything money could buy and parents distracted by the pressures of a deepening secular culture. Things in abundance and a spiritual vacuum! Meanwhile there has emerged a new awareness of the unity of man as the creation of God and a fresh sensitivity to human worth. Which is why Jesus Christ has become the Hero. He was the perfect human! In Him true humanness was expressed. He demonstrated what God meant man to be like when He created him. His humanness consisted in His unbroken fellowship with God, His total commitment to God's will, and His utter dependence upon His Heavenly Father. He gave priority to union with God. He came to do only what pleased God and He said, "I can do nothing by myself."

Apart from me you can do nothing.
—John 15:5

Friday

Personal relationships cannot be negotiated! They are seasoned and strengthened through struggle. We expect them to be automatic—just do what comes naturally and they will work out all right. We assume struggle is alien and tend to surrender and quit when the going gets tough. When, as a matter of fact, tough going is the raw material of the mature relationship.

Some, not willing to pay the price, capitulate to the first difficult situation, negotiation fails—they're through! Such people leave behind them a host of shallow friendships, marriages, business relationships—and broken dreams. The very difficulties that could have exercised their relationship, making it strong and durable, became the excuse for turning it in. The struggle that could have deepened and sweetened love was used as the justification for separation or divorce. The pressure that would have galvanized a business relationship became the excuse for dissolving it. "Coalitions cannot be negotiated—they are forged."*

Commitment is the key! Take the original covenant seriously, determine that the relationship must endure, and exclude divorce or dissolution as options. Quit acting like a spoiled child, pouting and whining when things do not go your way. Be mature. Put your values where they belong. Work at your relationships with Christ, wife, children, associates, neighbors, peers, men of another color, etc. Persons are infinitely more important than things!

> *What good is it for a man to gain the whole world, yet forfeit his soul?*
> —Mark 8:36

*Ebony

 Monday

Lack of knowing is not the problem. It's lack of doing! Most Christians know more than they do. They're not using their knowledge, not living it out in their lives. They are not incarnating the truth they profess. And to make matters worse, for some seeking more knowledge justifies inaction and non-involvement. Unused knowledge piles up, stagnates, sterilizes volition. Some make a career out of acquiring Bible knowledge, rarely translating into action the knowledge gained.

The ugliest manifestation of this is failure to love. The Scriptures are full of admonitions to love: "Dear friends, let us love one another, for love comes from God. Everyone who loves has been born of God and knows God. Whoever does not love does not know God" (1 John 4:7-8). The command of our Lord is explicit and clear. "Love your enemies, do good to those who hate you, bless those who curse you, pray for those who mistreat you" (Luke 6:27-28).

That is plain language! Yet there are those professing to follow Christ who have heads full of Bible knowledge and hearts empty of love. Preoccupied with piety and dogma, they blandly ignore and neglect their responsibility to love others. Seeing the disparity between their knowledge and their deeds, the world rejects their religion. The world is waiting for Christians to become Christian!

Why do you call me, 'Lord, Lord,' and do not do what I say? —Luke 6:46

 Tuesday

Christianity has not failed. It has not really been tried! Christians have failed when they have embraced a tradition which is something less than Jesus Christ propagated and equated it with the faith of Christ. It is far easier to live a moral life than it is to live a selfless life! Far easier to hang on selfishly to possessions and pleasures and to substitute morality for selflessness!

Authentic Christianity is infinitely more than morality. Atheists may be moral, especially if they have been reared with the benefits of a Judeo-Christian culture. Morality is not peculiar to Christianity. Christianity is basically selfless and God-centered. Christianity has a cross at its heart! Crossless Christianity is a contradiction! Which explains the impotence and irrelevance of much twentieth century religion which is labeled Christianity. Respectability has been equated with Christianity. Conviction has been compromised to conform to the status quo, reducing Christianity to a comfortable cult! (One synonym for respectability is mediocrity.)

Christian faith really begins when a man says "no" to self and "yes" to Jesus Christ. Christian faith is operative when others rather than self are paramount! The dynamic of Christianity is released only when ego is denied: as a grain of corn must die in the soil before it can produce; like a servant whose purpose is fulfilled when the master is pleased. Jesus said,

> *If anyone would come after me, he must deny himself and take up his cross and follow me.* —Matthew 16:24

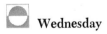 **Wednesday**

Every man has a god. Even the atheist! He

55

believes in No-god, and is often more zealous, more religious about his belief in No-god than some men who believe in God. It is not easy to have faith in No-god. Such a faith is held in the face of overwhelming evidence to the contrary. In fact, the only thing that "saves face" for the atheist is the fact of God's existence. Nobody would take an atheist seriously if there were no God. Any more than you would listen to someone who made a big deal out of proving there is no Santa Claus. Why pay attention to him who labors to disprove what is non-existent? God is! Therefore the atheist is not shadowboxing, not beating the air. He's conducting a real war against a real Opponent. The fact of God's existence is what gives the atheist status!

The real question is not whether a man believes in God or not, but what kind of a God does he serve? One man serves the god Mammon: Money is Everything! The whole weight of his life is thrown into the acquisition of Wealth. The more he gets, the more he wants. Enough is never. Mammon is a hard taskmaster, a merciless tyrant. It has destroyed many.

Another puts Pleasure first; he follows a giddy, shallow, senseless round of froth. He takes Pleasure wherever he finds it, hungrily devouring it like a starved animal tearing at a cadaver. The tragedy is that it takes more and more Pleasure to get less and less satisfaction. The point of diminishing return is reached quickly. Authentic delight decreases in inverse ratio to increased effort. The pitiful pay-off is a hollow life, emptiness, a bubble.

Still another serves the god Fame or Power or Prestige—or the worst tyrant of all, the god *self*—and inevitably reaps what he sows.

Man becomes like his god! He grows into the image of that which he worships. The wise man serves the true God, the God of our Lord and Savior Jesus Christ. What kind of a god do you serve?

> *Now this is eternal life: that men may know you, the only true God, and Jesus Christ, whom you have sent."*
> —John 17:3

 Thursday

Apparently some "Christians" simply have to be entertained. Watch them at a conference, for example: big names, well-known personalities, spectacular events draw the crowds. When it comes to the "nitty-gritty" of the real work, the exodus is massive.

One conference session I attended featured several international speakers, and some had difficulty communicating in English. Many walked out of the meeting. They were not even willing to listen, when listening was hard. Watch the meetings devoted to business and reports of the work; registered delegates stay away in droves. They plan social engagements instead.

Ironically, many of those who disengage themselves from the "shirt-sleeve" sessions are the most vocal in their profession of faith—and often the most critical. Give them scintillating speakers, dramatic events, prominent persons with whom to hobnob, and they'll be around. But when it comes to the work, "let George do it." If you want to keep some Christians happy, you must entertain them. They want to be counted in, but they cannot be counted on! The penetrating word of Jesus comes to mind,

> *Why do you call me 'Lord, Lord,' and do not what I say?*   —Luke 6:46

 Friday

Theological knowledge and spiritual maturity are not identical. One does not mature on the basis of accumulated religious data; he matures in terms of his obedience! It is possible to know a lot about the Bible and remain a spiritual infant. If the knowledge accumulated is not translated into action, there is no growth. In fact, this is one explanation for the spiritual adolescent; he became more interested in what he could learn than in what he could be. Spiritual truth is not intended simply to teach us something, but to make us something. Spiritual truth goes to the heart and the will more than to the head and the intellect.

One test for authentic Christian teaching is whether or not there is a decision to make. The word of truth always leads to personal verdict. A man can never be the same after hearing God's truth spoken in the power of God's Holy Spirit; he will either obey and go forward, or ignore and die a little. There's never anything merely academic in Jesus Christ. His words are always moral, always involve a personal issue, always demand action of some kind. To get sidetracked onto the merely academic in religion is to begin to deteriorate spiritually. Academic defection is as serious as moral defection in spiritual things!

This is why the spiritual life of some has crystallized and become static: a man becomes enamored with the purely intellectual aspects of theology and lets knowledge lead him away from an intimate, personal walk with the Savior. Interested more and more with what he can learn from the Bible, he becomes increasingly impressed with what he is learning, increasingly preoccupied with his growing knowledge of "deeper truth."

He begins to become aware of the subtle opinion that he is a superior intellectual.

The man who cultivates a close, obedient, personal relationship with Jesus Christ keeps healthily humble as he becomes increasingly aware of the disparity between his best and the matchless Lord he serves. And incidentally, he does not sacrifice knowledge by this proximity to Christ. He keeps knowledge in its place. His passion is to love Christ more and serve Him with greater effectiveness. What he is learning is always subordinate to what he is becoming.

Why do you call me, 'Lord, Lord,' and do not do what I say? —Luke 6:46

 Monday

What constitutes Christian character? What is its real criterion? Some make creed the final test; what a man believes is the thing. Creed is important: a man can't be a Christian if he believes wrongly about Christ. Christian character begins with right belief, but it doesn't stop there. It is possible to hold orthodox creed and live like the devil. The Bible says that "the devils believe, and tremble."

Others say conduct is the test. Watch how a man acts, and you can determine whether or not he is a Christian. But there are many non-Christians who are ethical. They follow some other religion, or no religion at all, and maintain high moral standards. Furthermore an evil man can order his conduct to achieve an evil purpose. He does nice things for bad ends. He may treat you well when his designs on you are wicked or, to say the least, selfish—like the man who gave a six-year-old girl a dime, lured her into his car, and ravished her. Just like a lot of business deals —same principle, different stakes.

It's not a new thing: acting like a good man until the stage is set to steal or exploit or kill. It's the strategy of the "confidence" game. Fact is, a great deal of life is like this today: sophisticated, respectable, polished, suave, but underneath the same hypocrisy. Buy a man a drink, take him to lunch, play golf with him (let him win), buy him a nice gift. Why? For his sake? No, for your own. He's got something you want.

The real test for Christian character is not creed or conduct or a lot of other things men judge by. The real test is one's motives. Not what one does, but why one does it! Motive is the thing to fear most. You can never trust a man with wrong motives, no matter how well he behaves. In fact, the finer his behavior, the more dangerous when falsely motivated. God is interested in motivation! Hence the tragedy of those who work so hard to make a living and don't know what they're living for!

The Lord sees not as man sees; man looks on the outward appearance, but the Lord looks on the heart. —1 Samuel 16:7

 Tuesday

Philosophers have a word for it: *summum bonum!* By which they mean the supreme good or the highest goal for man. What is the greatest thing toward which a man can strive? What goal, more than any other, will demand the best that is in a man? Every man is born with certain distinctive talent, ability, aptitude, capacity. What will most exploit these built-in values in a man? What will discover them, use them, turn them into blessing and benefit? What will get the most out of a man, make the most of him, prime him to be his creative best, reach maximum efficiency and highest productivity? Psychologists have developed many aptitude tests designed to help a man discover himself, but these tests are not infallible.

One of the deep, deep tragedies of life is the "might-have-been," the man who never lived up to his potential in life. He had it in him, but it was never discovered and used. Great ability buried and useless! He is the man who was made to soar in life; instead he hopped along like a bird with clipped wings. He reached the sunset of life to discover he could have been so much more than he was. First-class man, settling for second class. This is pitiful. It ought not be. It need not be!

A man's goal is everything! The higher the goal, the greater the man. It is the difference between achievement and failure. (Of course there is the man who reaches his goal only to discover that he didn't really achieve anything: He simply had such a low goal that he couldn't miss!) Often this little man with the low goal is consumed with pride by what he mistakes for success. Conceit is characteristic of the man with easy targets. Great men of God in another century asked this question: "What is the chief end of man?" Their answer: "Man's chief end is to glorify God and enjoy Him forever!" This is man at his best, destined to fulfill himself to the fullest. Man dedicated to God, putting Him first in all things.

Seek first his kingdom and his righteous-
ness.   —Matthew 6:33

 Wednesday

One thrilling fact stands out as you become familiar with the Bible. Though one fact among many, it is one of the most practical: God has a plan for your life! A wonderful plan, a perfect plan, a plan that takes into consideration all your aptitudes and talents, demands the most from you, and utilizes your ability to the outside edge. This plan will give you your highest degree of freedom, help you realize your maximum productivity, creativity, and efficiency. It will keep you at your best!

Israel was always happiest, most prosperous, when it followed God; and conversely, it always suffered a sharp decline in its prosperity, happiness, and productivity when it ceased from following God. Jesus' incarnation demonstrated this: a human body, filled with God, absolutely dedicated to the will of God. Jesus Christ came to do God's will. He spoke the words God gave Him, He did the deeds of God. He never vacillated one fraction nor one split second from this program of implicit obedience to the Heavenly Father. And the result was a perfectly balanced, perfectly integrated personality. Jesus was never the victim of His circumstances. He was always the master of them! He demonstrated what happens when God is in control!

Of course you and I can never measure up to Jesus Christ. But He is our goal, our model. He set the example. This does not mean that we try to imitate His ethics. That is impossible. It does mean we are to emulate Him in His out-and-out submission to God! It means we ought to live for much more important that a man examine himself inwardly with regard to his spiritual resources.

The question to ask oneself is this: how much am I worth, not in terms of possessions, but in terms of personality? It's not what a man has that counts, but what a man is. Not cash but character! The way to figure real worth is to look at the resources one has that cannot be taken away from him in a moment by some catastrophe. It's not how big a living a man makes, but what he's living for that gives the index to that man's true value. You judge a man not by where he comes from, but where he's going! Roger Babson said, "It is a crime for any man to be in any business that does not make the human race healthier and happier!" This is the real test of a man: what is his master motive, the dominant drive in his life? Where's he going?

This is the terrible, tragic perversion of the profit motive. Men make profit an end in itself. They measure success in terms of the size of a man's profit. And in twentieth-century America multiplied thousands of splendid men and women are mastered by the passion for profit. Profit is the test. Not what they produce, but how much they can make! Not whether or not the product benefits humanity, but whether or not it will make money. Profit becomes the be-all and end-all of life. Who can measure the utter, incredible, pathetic waste of some of the finest administrative and executive genius, some of the cream of American productive energy, dissipated without regard for anything but profit?

The good man, the godly man, makes a profit as a means to the end. His life is motivated by a far higher goal. He uses his profit to greater ends.

What really drives you day by day? Why all this "blood, sweat, and tears?" Take a long, honest look at your life. Let false motives drain away. Set your mind on the highest goal!

> *Seek first his kingdom and his righteousness.* —Matthew 6:33

 Friday

Get one big, basic question settled for yourself and you'll solve many of your problems, eliminate many more, and enjoy an over-all increase in personal efficiency. Ignore this question and you suffer serious consequences. You cut down your productivity and limp along through life when you ought to be a battering ram, a dynamo! Most men have so much more to offer than they really give. They are satisfied with so little output, utilize so little of their talent. They are the "might-have-beens," the cult of the "goof-off." This big question doesn't sound very impressive, but actually it is fundamental in its practical application.

It is the control factor in the life, the directive that gives the real push!

What are you living for?

Not how do you make a living? But what is the big drive, the major motive? What is your real life purpose? What's the big why behind everything you do? Are you one who works hard all day to make money to buy food to get strength to work hard to make more money to buy more food to get more strength to work harder to make money to buy food? Are you going in circles? Is life like a race track simply because you have never settled once-for-all your real goal for living? This is tragedy in the first magnitude! How can a man succeed in business if he doesn't know what he is in business for? And how can he make a success of living if he hasn't the slightest notion what he's living for?

Not only must a man have a life purpose, but it must be a high purpose, lest he accomplish his purpose only to discover that he hasn't done anything important in life. He achieved his goal not because he was successful, but because his goal was so low! For the man with a low goal, life is just a day to day affair. He may be a good man, but good for what? Nothing! Just a zero with the edges rubbed off! The world is no worse because of him, but it's no better either. He needs a purpose large enough to challenge him, draw the best out of him, demand his top efforts, utilize his full ability, capacity, and ingenuity. He me I believe this is right, although I would not necessarily feel it would be a rule for general application. Nevertheless, 'Do not store up for yourselves treasures on earth' (Matt. 6:19), and 'Seek ye first his kingdom and his righteousness' (Matt. 6:33), and 'A man's life does not consist in the abundance of his possessions' (Luke 12:15) all seem to be warnings against reliance upon money for security. Money simply is not security! It is the nearest thing to 'coined labor' that I know, but it can be stolen, eroded by inflation, confiscated for governmental purposes, frozen by law, or eliminated by war.

"In other words, it does not provide a hedge against any of the things which people fear. The only security is a life lived for Jesus Christ and held 'in the hollow of His hand,' and the only safe investment is giving all possible money to the Lord! Proof? 'But store up for yourselves treasures in heaven, where moth and rust do not destroy, and where thieves do not break in and steal' (Matt. 6:20). 'One man gives freely, yet grows all the richer; another withholds what he should give, and only suffers want' (Prov. 11:24). 'Cast your bread upon the waters, for you will find it after many days' (Prov. 11:1). 'Give, and it will be given to you, a good measure, pressed down, shaken together and running over, will be poured into your lap. For with the measure you use, it will be measured to you' (Luke 6:38). God helped me to learn in my heart these great les-

sons I had learned in my head. Not my money
only, Lord, but my whole self also—for Your good
pleasure—to do with as You will. Here am I—
God use me!"

> *For from him (God) through him and to
> him are all things. To him be the glory
> forever! Amen.*   —Romans 11:36

 Tuesday

Man has "come of age" they say. The very pride
and presumption which makes such a claim is its
denial! Maturity doesn't call attention to itself—
doesn't need to. Boasting of one's maturity is a
sign of puberty. Modern man has all the "ear-
marks" of adolescence! Wholesale repudiation of
the past—that is adolescence. Acute case of inde-
pendence—that is adolescence. The new morality?
Clearly a child's break with parental discipline.

One of the most "sophisticated" publishers of
our day admitted to an interviewer that he was
motivated by a strong desire to "thumb his nose
at the moral strictures of his devout parents." And
he's become a millionaire in the last ten years by
pandering to his revolt! That is adolescence! Sophisticated? Yes. Mature? No! Modern man is
smart, but he is not wise.

Of course there are many mature men on the

contemporary scene, for which we can be profoundly grateful. But the spirit of the age is adolescence, in the church as well as in the world. Take the short-lived "death of God" theology for example. That was adolescence in a most obvious form. Its exponents may have been intellectual, but it was the intellectualism of the sophomore (nobody's smarter than the sophomore). Such hypertrophy of the intellect is characteristic of the young man who has just begun to think for himself and compulsively jettisons the old ideas.

> *And you, Capernaum, will you be lifted up to the skies? No, you will go down to the depths. If the miracles that were performed in you had been performed in Sodom, it would have remained to this day. But I tell you that it will be more bearable for Sodom on the day of judgment than for you. . . . I praise you, Father, Lord of heaven and earth, because you have hidden these things from the wise and learned, and revealed them to little children.*
> —Matthew 11:23-25

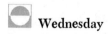 **Wednesday**

Then there is the man who wanted change. So

impatient was he for change that he was unable to stay at one task long enough to implement his revolutionary ideas. If the situation didn't conform to his dreams instantly, he looked for other worlds to conquer and blamed the system for its failure. The trouble was always with something else, someone else. He was always right! So he kept moving from one thing to another in pursuit of his goals, with the result that the only thing that changed was his geography. The only thing that moved was himself! He left behind a string of half-baked programs and some heartbroken, disillusioned followers. He is a bitter, cynical, self-righteous, against-the-world hypocrite!

Someone has said, "It is better to bring one man home than to leave three men on bases." Change is needed; no thoughtful person disputes that. But changers are needed also! Men who not only have the vision, but the patience to work at it, wait for it. One of the strange facts of our day is the man who is so critical of the rhetoric of others, who is constantly demanding action, yet who never acts himself—never puts his life where his mouth is. He must figure loudness is as relevant as action for himself. He says so much more than he does. And when he runs out of hearers, he looks for other suckers. Jesus said,

> *No one who puts his hand to the plow and looks back is fit for service in the kingdom of God.* —Luke 9:62

It's easy to know what to do when you don't have to do it! Easy to make decisions when yours is not the responsibility to decide. One interesting and aggravating phenomenon of our time is the vocal critic who always has the answers. He always knows the way to go and never has to go himself! Always knows what to do and never has to do it!

These are the "experts" who pontificate on every conceivable issue. Free from the responsibility of following through on their decisions, they tell those who have the responsibility what to do. What a difference between the spectator in the bleachers who criticizes the way the game goes and the player on the field who must play the game. "Drugstore quarterbacks" never make any mistakes!

This does not mean dissent is wrong, of course. Dissent is the stuff of which democracy is made. But the spirit of the dissenter is the thing. Let the spirit of the critic be sensitive to the burden of decision borne by the one criticized.

> . . . *in the same way you judge others,*
> *you will be judged. . . . Why do you look*
> *at the speck of sawdust in your brother's*
> *eye and pay no attention to the plank in*
> *your own eye?* —Matthew 7:2-3

Friday

You wouldn't stand for insubordination in your business or home, nor can you run a business, a home, or anything else if those involved will not abide by the established order, will not "knuckle under" to authority. Even sports events demand that players follow the rules. The rule breakers, the insubordinates, the anarchists foul up the best-laid plans.

This is unalterably true in every area of life: productivity, efficiency, and fulfillment are possible only when there is obedience and cooperation. Any system, however cleverly organized, breaks down under anarchy. Yet there are intelligent men living in God's world who act as though they can ignore the Lord of the universe, disregard His order, transgress His rules, and still have an efficient, tranquil, productive world. Men who wouldn't tolerate rebellion in their business for five minutes often operate with utter disregard for the Divine Management.

Revolt is revolt whether it is militant, blatant rebellion or quiet, respectable indifference. A child who ignores the rules is just as insubordinate as one who fights them. No father can tolerate a son who continues to disregard family interests. Men don't have to sabotage a plant—they can just sit down or slow down and the result will be as devastating so far as production is concerned! And a man does not have to take a blasphemous, profane stand against God and the moral order to upset the balance of life either. He can just go on living as though God doesn't make any difference!

Being ethical is not enough if the ethical man ignores his accountability to God and lives as though he has no vertical responsibility in life. This is anarchy. Spiritual anarchy! This is the basic deception in secularism: treating religion as simply a man to man proposition, paying no heed whatever to the God-man relationship. The good man who is godless is the real problem!

> *All we like sheep have gone astray; we have turned every one to his own way.*
> —Isaiah 53:6

 Monday

The most desperate need of our day is spiritual and moral renewal—not social revolution. Not that they are mutually exclusive, nor that we should neglect social obligation while we seek revival. But social revolution without spiritual and moral renewal is illusion! Replacing the status quo (however degenerate) with chaos is irrational.

Russia represents the most successful revolution

of our day (they've been at it sixty years), yet her leaders continue to aspire to standards and conditions long since realized and improving in the U.S.A., and to which end Russia has been continually modifying her revolutionary policy to conform to American practice. Not that we do not have a long way to go in resolving social and economic inequity. But revolution does not dissolve prejudice, greed, avarice, and selfishness in the human heart. Spiritual and moral renewal will!

It must begin with the church, with Christians, with you and me! We cannot generate renewal; it cannot be "worked up" by human effort and ingenuity. But we can desire it. We can seek it. We can acknowledge our need for it. We can confess the selfishness and indifference among us and within us which have contributed to the deterioration of the spiritual and moral life of our nation. We can stop deploring and blaming and criticizing and start humbling ourselves before Almighty God and praying for forgiveness and healing and awakening. We can offer ourselves to Christ as agents of His reconciliation and then begin to close the gap between our profession of Christianity and our practice. We can ask for a fresh baptism of the love of God by the Spirit of God and serve Christ as we serve others.

Wilt thou not revive us again, that thy people may rejoice in thee?
—Psalm 85:6

Tuesday

What is man? What is humanness? What does it mean to be truly human? The clue is the will!

God created man with the freedom of choice. His destiny depended upon his use of this freedom. Satan's subtle subterfuge in the first temptation was to raise a false issue: "Eat this fruit and you will be like gods, knowing good from evil." He made the issue knowing good from evil; the vital option was to eat or not to eat. To eat was to disobey God; to refuse was to obey. Satan confused the issue by cloaking evil in a good and desirable garment. What a temptation—knowledge!

This is the deepest issue in history: whether a man chooses to obey or disobey God; whether or not he will conform his will to God's. (Many evade this issue by denying the reality of God or by denying that God has spoken.) To obey God is to be human in the fullest, finest, primary sense! To refuse to obey is to deprave humanness.

Jesus Christ was the perfect man! His perfection consisted in His total and complete submission to the Father's will, His uninterrupted obedience to God. That was the real issue in the wilderness temptation! Jesus came "to do the will of God." He said, "I do only that which pleases Him." That's humanity as God intended! Obey God and be a man!

Therefore, I urge you, brothers, in view

of God's mercy, to offer yourselves as living sacrifices, holy and pleasing to God—which is your spiritual worship.

                              —Romans 12:1

 Wednesday

The greatest need of our day is for those who profess faith in Christ to begin living as though they do! Instead of lusting after some new truths, we should begin to practice what we already know. Our trouble is that our knowledge is so far ahead of our deeds. We need to catch up. Potentially the most revolutionary force in America is Christians when they start living up to what they say they believe.

Knowing the Bible for the sake of knowing the Bible is a dead end. When we who know the Bible repent of our failure to live up to what we know and start conforming to its precepts, we will release the most powerful, purifying, reconciling, redemptive force in history. We don't need to be taught something new; we need to be reminded of what we already know.

Jesus said, "Love your enemies." That's good for beginners. Jesus said, "Blessed are the peacemakers." Jesus said, "Do good to them that abuse you." Jesus said, "The cares of this world, the deceitfulness of riches, and the lust for other things, choke the word of God in a man's heart." Jesus said, "Do not be anxious about tomorrow, what you shall eat, or drink, or wear." By His grace, let's decide to do it!

> *Seek first his kingdom and his righteousness.* —Matthew 6:33

 Thursday

Jesus Christ did not die to save America! Nor did He die to save capitalism. He did not give His life to preserve any human system or organization or institution. He died for sinners: American sinners, European sinners, Asian sinners, Latin American sinners, African sinners—white, black, red, and yellow sinners! Christ died for all—all sinners!

There is no biblical justification for equating the kingdom of God with any human civilization, culture, nation, system, or institution. When Jesus Christ returns to establish His perfect kingdom, it will be utterly new, radically different, totally other than any originated by man.

Loyalty to Christ and His kingdom transcends all allegiance. His kingdom is universal, righteous, divine. Followers of Christ ought to put their priorities in order and give allegiance to their Lord. In World War II, Nazi soldiers bore on their belt buckles the inscription "Gott mit uns." They were defeated; God was not! It was simply the end of the Third Reich. People who speak and act and pray as though their status quo is to be preserved eternally need to wake up to the hard facts. God has planned something infinitely better.

> *Seek first his kingdom and his righteousness.* —Matthew 6:33

 Friday

An unbalanced spiritual diet has serious consequences! Take the person who indulges only in truth which caters to his whims, reads only self-pleasing parts of the Bible, preoccupies himself with ideas which leave his status quo undisturbed —the person who has no "stomach" for the "whole counsel of God." "Having itching ears," such a person listens only when the teacher gives him what he enjoys. Let a speaker fail to conform, deviate from the favored line, and the ears close and the mind rests. Hearing he hears not, and if the unpleasant theme persists, another teacher is sought. Like a glutton, he craves to feast on light, rich, pleasant, exotic spiritual morsels; and the more pre-digested, the better. He doesn't grow strong; he just gets spiritually fat, soft, slothful, and apathetic.

People like this rarely join a church—they join a preacher. They make a career of listening, and they become professional critics.

"Preach love," says one, "I don't like judgment." He has no appetite for the strong meat of righteousness, not to mention the fact that he really doesn't understand love. He has sentimentalized it beyond recognition. Character is the backbone of love, and character means virtue. Virtue repudiates unrighteousness; it is a consistent judgment upon it.

"The Sermon on the Mount is my religion," says another. By which he generally means some thoughts he has sifted from "The Sermon" which delight his fancy, carefully avoiding hard truth which rebukes his apathy or challenges his status quo. Often in this category is the man who will "take Jesus" but rejects the "Christ of Paul." (As though there were a difference.)

"Preach grace" urges another. Works have no place in his appetite. Ephesians is his book (parts of it that is), but away with James. Tell him that a man is saved by grace, but don't spoil it by reminding him that grace which saves generates works which become the sons of God.

Announce a series on Daniel or Revelation, and the crowd comes. Dig into the ethics of God's Word, discuss the strong meat of man's duty, and the crowd thins out perceptibly. "Johnny on the spot" for prophecy, but interest lags otherwise.

What a choice vessel unto the Lord is the man who takes the whole Word of God as his counsel; who doesn't flinch when truth penetrates and demands a verdict of personal commitment; who chews patiently the meat of the Word and obeys! Who "endures hardness as a good soldier of Jesus Christ."

> *He cuts off every branch in me that bears*
> *no fruit.* —John 15:2

 Monday

"There is something worse than wanting things and not having the means to get them; it's having the means and not wanting anything." Thus one Christian businessman revealed the monotony and boredom of his life when he had achieved everything he sought only to discover he remained desperately unsatisfied. Satiated but unsatisfied! He had reached the terrible barrenness of luxury, overstuffed and still hungry. The harder he tried, the hungrier he got for a reality which eluded him like vapor while it continued to tease and lure him. He discovered money could not buy the things he wanted most in life: the love of his wife, self-respect, the peace of God. He had money to buy anything he wanted, but he didn't want anything his money could buy! And he desperately longed for intangibles which remained inexpressible, indefinable, and aloof.

He got his answer in Jesus Christ! Literally! In the midst of his spiritual bankruptcy, face to face with the incalculable poverty of a life that had everything and still did not have what he wanted, he quietly knelt beside his wife and the two of them opened their hearts to Jesus Christ. The miracle happened! They fell in love all over again and the spectre of divorce vanished. For years he had tried to stop drinking but the desire for liquor enslaved him; now the taste left and never returned. For the first time in his life the Bible was meaningful and he wanted to go to church. He had been awakened to the glorious fact that Jesus Christ is the only One who can really satisfy a man; that when Jesus Christ is Lord, everything else in a man's life has meaning and value in the right proportions.

> *He who has the Son has life; he who does not have the Son of God does not have life.* —1 John 5:12

 Tuesday

Secondhand faith is an anomaly! Christian faith

cannot be inherited, though its benefits are, which is the crux of moral disintegration. The modern American who enjoys all the benefits of Christian faith while at the same time ignoring that faith is like a prodigal son, who having long since used up the interest of a father's inheritance is now squandering the capital. And to compound the problem, he is making no spiritual and moral deposit for subsequent generations. His legacy to his progeny is spiritual bankruptcy! Such men are spiritual parasites, living off the benefits of the faith of former generations, depleting the moral capital of their generation, and robbing posterity of the benefits so richly enjoyed by themselves.

One evidence of this present-day spiritual profligacy is the fact that men take the benefits of religious dedication for granted. Our civilization is not automatic! It was born out of a deep and abiding faith in God, a sense of accountability to Him, and an awareness of His overruling providence in the affairs of men. Moral purity is the fruit of which spiritual dedication is the root! Reject the root and loss of the fruit is inevitable!

"The political and social practices of our civilization derive from their Christian content, and they will not long survive unless they are replenished by that faith. Practice unsupported by belief is a wasting asset."*

"... reason and experience both forbid us to

*Arnold J. Toynbee

expect that national morality can prevail in exclusion of religious principle."*

"The terrible things that are happening in some parts of the world are due to the fact that political and social practices have been separated from spiritual content."*

"Many laymen are living in the twilight of their parents' religion. When the twilight is past, they will be in complete darkness unless they make the vital ideals of their parents a part of their own experiences."*

> *Seek first his kingdom and his righteousness.* —Matthew 6:33

*George Washington
*John Foster Dulles
*Dr. Arthur L. Bietz, from "Incentives,"
  Christian Men, Inc.

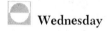 **Wednesday**

Middle-age hunger can be terrifying, especially when a man can't find a way to satisfy it. At middle age a man is relatively mature, relatively successful, relatively secure. Many of his early goals have been reached and the future is relatively predictable. The family is relatively grown, the marriage is relatively settled, life is relatively routine. The man has been places, seen things, done the usual, experienced the average ups and downs of life. He doesn't have quite the energy he used to, lacks the "get up and go," the drive and thrust, the resilience of earlier years. He's a little more sophisticated, plays it cool, takes things in stride. He's calmer, softer, slower, steadier, wiser, more efficient, more capable, more realistic, more sensible; he gets things done with less effort, fewer wasted strokes, less energy expended on trivia. He is more effective and productive. In a sense he's "arrived," and the most he can look forward to is just the same thing—only more of it.

Then comes the strange appetite—gnawing, stubborn, insatiable. Some try working harder, getting busier, but the hunger persists. Some drink more, but that isn't the answer. Some get involved in extra-curricular activities—club, golf, trapshooting, etc.—but these do not satisfy. Another seeks satisfaction in extra-marital adventures. Convention time is play-around-with-the-women time. He tries to prove he's still a man, still attractive, still a "lady killer." The kickback is worse than the hunger.

Trouble is, he's looking in the wrong places. He's not hungry for variety—he's hungry for reality! He's God hungry! And only God will satisfy. Jesus Christ is the perfect satisfaction for middle-age hunger. Jesus Christ guarantees fulfillment. The middle-aged man who is fed up will find delicate and palatable food through faith in the Son of God.

> *I am come that they may have life, and have it to the full.* —John 10:10

 Thursday

Dr. Norman Vincent Peale tells of an experience he had when asked to address a thousand business and professional men in a Michigan city. He was seated beside a psychiatrist, and during their conversation the doctor pointed to the crowd of men saying, "There's real tragedy! There are the finest men in the world, but they are dying men, dying with fear and resentment, going to pieces with the pressures of modern living. Tell these men," the doctor continued, "that there is only one physician in the world who can help them. He is the great physician! Tell them that is from a man who has practiced medicine in Michigan for forty years."

This is the tragedy of modern America! Some of the finest people in business, industry, and the professions, some of the top executive geniuses, are going to pieces because of inner pressures. There can be no real health in the body until there is peace in the soul! How many have gone to their physician for a diagnosis only to be told there is nothing physically wrong. And yet they are losing their grip, their drive, their sharp edge.

Learn a lesson from Jesus Christ Himself! No matter how confused the circumstances, regardless of how the noisy, angry, hate-infused mob swirled about Him, He was always the Master of the situation! Because He was right where it really matters! He had peace of soul! He was right deep down inside Himself. There was no division, no disintegration, no tension. He was right with God! That is absolutely fundamental! Because no matter how peaceful things are around a man, he is never really peaceful until there is peace within his soul. And conversely, no matter how confusing, tense, or maddening circumstances are on the outside, the man who has God's peace within is always the master.

Settle this now! No man is strong who does not have inner strength, who does not have subterranean resources that come from God. He may look rugged, but pressures will make him crack up, cave in. It's what's inside that counts! Jesus Christ is the only One who can give a man this! He lived, died, rose again from the dead, and settled the sin question. He conquered it once for all! Conquered it for every man who will put his trust in Him, follow Him, let Him be the Lord of his life. That man is invincible who makes

Christ Lord of his life. Let Jesus Christ rule your life! Let His peace fill your soul.

> *Peace I leave with you; my peace I give you. I do not give to you as the world gives.* —John 14:27

 Friday

"Whatever you make the issue, you make the idol." Spoken by a former revered teacher, that statement illuminates the cause of much of the confusion in the church today. We have sanctified controversy, often in the name of peace. If one is not divisive, he is not prophetic! Economic, social, and political views have been elevated to absolutes—which Jesus Christ has been made a tool to support. He is proclaimed as a proponent of totally divergent positions, the holders of which categorically place each other under His judgment. Loyalty to Christ is equated with opposing claims. Disagreement is tantamount to treason.

Jesus Christ is not on the side of any human system! "As high as the heaven is above the earth, so high are His ways above ours, His thoughts above ours." Every economic, social, and political system is infinitely subordinate to His transcendent, eternal purpose. We certainly will never have

peace if we persist in identifying our cause with
His and demanding that all agree or be condemned. By whatever name, that is the anatomy
of war!

Jesus said,
My kingdom is not of this world.
—John 18:36
*Seek first his kingdom and his righteous-
ness.* —Matthew 6:33

 Monday

"How can a man be born when he is old?" A
legitimate question in the light of Jesus' statement
to Nicodemus, "You must be born again!" Jesus
had an answer! First He made it clear that the
new birth is a mystery. ("The wind blows wherever it pleases. You may hear its sound, but you
cannot tell where it comes from or where it goes.
So it is with everyone born of the Spirit" (John
3:8). This does not mean it is irrational; it is
supra-rational. Failure to understand the new birth
does not disqualify a man; neither does it mean
that the new birth is unreal. It simply means that
it is the work of God and therefore outside man's
intellectual comprehension. But though the new
birth cannot be explained, it can be experienced!
(You may not know where the wind comes from

or where it's going, but you know it's blowing.) A man can be born again without knowing how it works.

What does a man do to be born of God? Of first importance, there is no "one" or "only" method for a man to be born of God. Jesus said simply "Come unto Me." Anyone who responds to that simple invitation will be met by God. Furthermore, a man ought to realize the new birth is not something he can do for himself. The new birth is not a human invention. It is the work of God alone! The fact is God will do this work for any man who desires it. The only requirement for the new birth is willingness. In other words, the key problem between God and man is man's unwillingness. This the Bible treats as sin, the bottom sin! There's something in man's will that poisons him toward God, makes him revolt against godliness. He wants to be moral and respectable but without surrendering himself to God. Among intelligent, respectable men this revolt usually expresses itself through indifference. The man who thinks (or lives as though) he doesn't need God is a godless man, whatever his religion, theology, or ethical standard.

Basically, repentance is a change of mind whereby a man decides he needs God. Conversion is the follow-through as the man, acting on his decision, turns to God for help, for forgiveness, for new life. When a man does this, God meets him with the gift of a new life. This is how it works. Try it and see for yourself.

> *To all who received him (Christ), to those who believed in his name, he gave the right to become children of God.*
> —John 1:12

 Tuesday

Prayer is not soliloquy! Prayer is conversation with a real Person who actually hears what is prayed and does something about it. Of course prayer has subjective value; it blesses the one who prays. If a man never got an answer, he would be a better man for having bowed his knees to Almighty God. A man "never stands taller than when he kneels to God." But prayer is of infinitely more value than what it means to the one who prays. Prayer is objective as well as subjective.

Prayer brings results, not just in the man who prays, but in the ones for whom he prays, the things for which he prays. A man prays in his home in America for a missionary friend in Africa; God hears the man in America and responds by supplying the need in Africa. That is prayer in the biblical sense. Anything less is a caricature of prayer as understood by the apostles, the patriarchs, and Jesus Himself.

Abraham did not pray for his own edification; he prayed for a son as did his wife Sarah. God gave them Isaac. Moses was utterly indifferent to his own welfare when he prayed. He was concerned for the children of Israel. God heard Moses and blessed Israel in the wilderness. Hannah prayed for a son. God heard her, and Samuel was born. Hannah prayed, and God gave Israel a great prophet to lead her into national prominence. Elijah prayed for rain, the rain came, and the Apostle James declared that it was Elijah's prayer that was responsible for the rain.

Prayer is not a soliloquy or a monologue. It is dialogue between man and God. When men pray sincerely, God responds. The Bible does not explain prayer, but it abounds with demonstrations of it. Have you really tried prayer? Before you scoff, try it! Jesus said,

> *(Men) should always pray and not give*
> *up.* —Luke 18:1

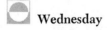 **Wednesday**

"Do I have a right to expect God to hear me now when I haven't prayed for years?" These words were spoken by the Washington representative of a large corporation while he was in the hospital with a serious and discouraging illness. Implicit in the question is the false notion that man can only expect from God that which he merits—that a man must somehow earn God's favor. Because this man had not bothered to pray for years, he assumed that he had no right to pray now.

This idea of Christianity is not uncommonly held, but it is contrary to the teaching of the Bible. It is a caricature of faith. At the heart of Christian faith is "grace." "Grace" by definition is "unmerited favor." That is, God does for man what he does not deserve and gives to man that of which he is unworthy. God always meets a man at the point of his need, however deep and complicated that need, when man looks to God for aid.

Of course this man felt strange about prayer, but the strangeness was on his part, not God's. Naturally prayer was unnatural, for the man was in new territory. But God had not forsaken him. The man had been ignoring God for years, despite God's constant nearness and continuing availability. God was a stranger to the man, but the man was no stranger to God. God knew him like an open book, loved him with an everlasting love, and had been waiting for years for that moment when the man had enough need to make him pray. The remarkable thing about Christian faith is that the moment a man turns to God in trust, or need, no matter how long he has been alienated, God meets him in love and grace. Jesus said,

> *Come to me, all you who are weary and burdened, and I will give you rest.*
> —Matthew 11:28

 Thursday

Do you demand an answer when you pray or do you seek God in prayer? Are you primarily interested in the gifts or in the Giver? Spiritual lust looks for answers; true piety seeks the Lord!

A great deal that we call prayer, stripped from its pious phraseology, is nothing more than dictating to God. It is not asking at all; it is ordering. It is treating God like a personal servant whose primary responsibility (duty) is to look after our affairs. And we usually pout and whine and complain when the answers are not forthcoming immediately.

Of course we would never admit this to ourselves, let alone to others. We just behave this way! Being proficient in the use of pious lingo, we say all the right things, but our attitude and conduct betray personal pique.

Authentic devotion leaves the answers with God.

Not that it is indifferent to answers; it simply rests in the transcendent wisdom, the deathless love, the everlasting care, and the unfailing grace of the Heavenly Father. It is preoccupied with the Giver rather than the gift. Its highest, deepest, largest satisfaction is the Father as He is known in the Son by the Spirit. True devotion can be satisfied with nothing less than the Lord Himself!

> *Fear not, Abram, I am your shield; your reward shall be very great.* —Genesis 15:1

 Friday

Do you always have to have the last word? After God speaks, must you say something? Something that takes the edge off God's Word, that whittles it down to man-size reasoning? How prone we are to take God's Word and pick away at it, rationalizing until the message we get is not worthy of God. If it were just human wisdom, God needn't have spoken it! Common sense is fine, but we don't need God for that. He gave us common sense, but He never intended that it become an enemy of His Word.

Do you take a splendid promise from the Bible, and emasculate it with your "intelligent" qualifications? Or do you ponder it, let its immense truth sink in and saturate your soul with God's truth? Do you listen or question? Obey or argue? Why bother with the Bible if all you do is debate with God, eliminating everything that doesn't square with your logic? Why consider the promises of God, if when you get through working them over they are reduced to human value? If you are unwilling to take God's Word at face value, why pretend to be a follower of Him who declared Himself to be the truth? God's Word does not depend upon your acceptance, but the peace of God in your heart depends upon God's Word! The strength and reassurance of the Word of God is wasted on the man whose intellectual pride makes him critical and skeptical.

There is no standard for measuring the incalculable loss to the man who refuses to take God at His Word; nor is there any way of expressing the immeasurable benefit to the man who takes the Bible seriously! Be silent when God speaks even when you doubt; give His Word a chance to grip you and validate itself in your mind and heart. It will! If you are "from Missouri" and must be shown, be willing and God will prove the utter reliability of His promises. Thomas doubted and received overwhelming evidence; and Jesus has never repulsed a "doubting Thomas." It is only the man who rationalizes and refuses proof who misses this blessing.

If a man chooses to do God's will, he will

find out whether my teaching comes from God. —John 7:17

Monday

Jesus Christ is the final, absolute, incontrovertible ground for Christian faith. If He can be discredited, Christianity is discredited. If He is wrong, Christianity is wrong. If He can fail, Christianity will fail! Christian faith rises or falls with Jesus Christ! Not our doctrine about Him, but Jesus Christ Himself. Our doctrine is fallible; He is not. Our doctrine may be wrong; He is not.

Put all the theology together—every thought man has ever formulated about Jesus Christ. He is greater by infinity than the sum total of all dogma conceived by the mind of man. You cannot escape Jesus Christ as a fact of history. He was actually born in a certain place at a certain time under certain conditions. He lived a certain kind of life, taught many things, did many things, and finally died as a common criminal in the method most accepted in that day for capital punishment. History is divided by Him. In the words of Charles Malik of Lebanon, "Jesus Christ is the hinge of history."

The fact of Jesus Christ's existence is indisputable, but the minute you accept Him as a fact of history, you cannot explain Him on any other grounds than that He was God in the flesh! He was unique in His birth. He was unique in His life. He was unique in His death. He was unique in His victory over death—the resurrection. What more reasonable response to Jesus Christ than that of doubting Thomas, who cried, "My Lord and my God."

> *Salvation is found in no one else; for there is no other name under heaven given to men by which we must be saved.*   —Acts 4:12

 Tuesday

The late C. S. Lewis of England was a "church-baiting agnostic" before his conversion to Christ following World War II. He once wrote: "Either Jesus Christ was what he claimed or he was a liar, and we should repudiate him. Or if he was not what he claimed to be, and not a liar, he was a madman and we should treat him as such. Or he was what he claimed to be and we should worship him."

Reduced to simplest terms, that is the issue! Either one goes all the way with Jesus Christ, or he should reject Him as a fraud or a fool. There

History is divided by His life into BC and AD. Every time you date a letter, you acknowledge Him. He is the dividing line of history, the center of time. His teaching was revolutionary. "Never man spake like this man." His ethics were the highest ever given. He spoke with absolute authority on every subject. His life was exemplary. He was the epitome of virtue. All goodness and greatness converged in His matchless Person. He suffered the injustice of an ignominious trial, the humiliation of a cruel death on a cross, capital punishment's most hideous device. (History's strangest paradox: The perfect man condemned as a criminal.) Three days after they put His body in a tomb, sealed it with a Roman seal, and stationed a platoon of soldiers about it, the seal was broken, the body gone. According to the testimony of more than five hundred people, He was seen on many occasions for forty days following this event.

Men everywhere, in all generations, agree as touching the greatness of Jesus Christ, His life and teachings. Yet everywhere men stubbornly ignore Him, reject Him, blaspheme Him in their daily conversation. Why? He claimed to be God. He did not say He was like God or a prophet of God, but He said He was God. He said to reject Him was to reject God. He said to dishonor Him was to dishonor God. He insisted that obedience to His teaching constituted the only dependable foundation for life and that to disobey Him was like building on sand. He said that men who did not accept Him would die in their sins and that a man's eternal destiny depended upon what that man did with Him. "Whoever does not believe (in him) stands condemned already because he has not believed" (John 3:18). He said He was going to rise from the dead and that this would be the supreme sign that He was what He claimed. His resurrection is one of the most solidly established facts of history! He is not a dead hero! To millions living today, Christ is a living reality, a contemporary Savior and Lord.

> *These are written that you may believe that Jesus is the Christ, the Son of God, and that by believing you may have life in his name.* —John 20:31

 Thursday

Demolition! Right on sophisticated Connecticut Avenue in the heart of the nation's capital. Total destruction is the prospect as the huge office building disappears. That's progress! An obsolete building is going down; soon a gleaming new structure of concrete, steel, and glass will rise in its place. That's the way of progress in the lives of buildings and men!

And it's the way of maturity in the Christian life as well. Some men never grow spiritually because they cling to the old. They will not die, will not mortify the flesh, will not submit to crucifixion. Christian growth for such a man is self-improvement at best. He equates spiritual maturation with remodeling and repair. He keeps busy shoring up, patching up, painting up the old life. He will not accept Christ's way of transformation, the way of drastic change. He desires the new, but he will not let go of the old. He wants the best that Christ offers, but he settles for the best that he can do. He'd like the new model, but he keeps repairing the old.

Christ's way is death to the old, assent to the new! Jesus said, "If anyone would come after me, he must deny himself and take up his cross and follow me" (Matt. 16:25). Paul said, "I have been crucified with Christ and I no longer live, but Christ lives in me" (Gal. 2:20).

Unless a kernel of wheat falls to the ground and dies, it remains only a single seed. —John 12:24

 Friday

As one reads the gospel narrative, he becomes

aware that men responded many different ways to Jesus Christ. Much the same as men respond today. See if you can find yourself among them.

There were at least four circles of men who followed Jesus, from those on the fringe of interest to those close in. Their influence for Christ was in inverse ratio to their distance from Christ. Beginning at the outer edge, farthest from Jesus, was the multitude. They were drawn to Him by many different magnets. Some were compelled by curiosity. They'd heard about Him and couldn't resist following to see what He had. Others were drawn by a whimsical interest in the work He was doing. Much as spectators at a game, they surrounded Him to see what He would do next, to be entertained. This was the extent of their interest! Some came for selfish reasons. They needed help and came to Jesus like a man runs to a fire escape, to get a way out of difficulty. Some hated the despotic pressure of Roman militarism and saw in Jesus a possible leader of rebellion. Still others went along, as many men do today, just to get on the bandwagon! But for whatever reason these men followed Jesus, they soon quit Him, soon turned back! They weren't willing to pay a price for righteousness! When they couldn't see anything in it for themselves, they rejected Him! Needless to say, the influence of such men was zero in the world so far as He was concerned.

There was a second circle closer in—the 120

main in you, ask whatever you wish, and
it will be given you. —John 15:7

 Monday

Jesus Christ was so irrelevant that they crucified Him! The religionists of His day would have
had to revise their confessions to accept Him.
They expected a Messiah who would deliver them
out of their dilemma brought on by the strong
hand of Rome. Jesus refused to mount a revolution against the status quo, so they rejected Him
—killed Him!

His failure to conform to their "system" brought
the wrath of the religious establishment down
upon Him. And this perversity was not peculiar
to Jesus' contemporaries. Ecclesiastical profession-
als have been doing it to Him ever since. Accus-
ing those who disagree with them of identifying
Jesus with their own set ways, religious "authori-
ties" justify their entrenched policies on the
grounds of "enlightened" understanding of Jesus.
Men keep trying to get Jesus to solve man's problems man's way, establishing their own criterion
for relevance. They reject Jesus if He will not
conform.

It was the judgment of Jesus' contemporaries
that He was irrelevant, and many religious men

today agree. To satisfy the religious men of His day, Christ would have had to forsake the cross: "Come down from the cross, if you are the Son of God!" (Matt. 27:40). To satisfy the thief, He would have had to save Himself: "Aren't you the Christ? Save yourself and us!" (Luke 23:39). He just couldn't win!

> *My teaching is not my own. It comes from him who sent me. If a man chooses to do God's will, he will find out whether my teaching comes from God or whether I speak on my own.* —John 7:16-17

Tuesday

A businessman brought a friend to the office to discuss Christian faith. This friend was quite belligerent about religion in general and Christianity in particular. He'd made up his mind against it! It was a lot of nonsense as far as he was concerned, a fact he made known in rather strong language. When he had had opportunity to let off enough steam to calm down, we led the conversation around to his reasons for such hostility in order to discover why he was so completely antagonistic. Among other things he said something like this: "We've had Christianity for 2000 years and look at the h—— of a mess the world's in! If your religion were any good it would work. I can't go for anything that doesn't work any better than Christianity!"

"Do you believe in medicine?" I asked him.

"Of course I do!"

"Would you consult a doctor or go to a hospital if you were ill?"

"Sure," he replied.

"In other words you think medicine is a good thing?"

"Naturally," he grunted.

Then it was pointed out to him that we have had the medical profession in the tradition of Hippocrates since 200 years before Christ, yet there is still much disease and sickness in the world.

"That's different," he countered, "medicine doesn't work unless you apply it. You've got to take it to make it work!"

Precisely! And you've got to take Christianity to make it work too! Christianity has not been tried and found inadequate. The trouble is that men have refused to try it. Jesus Christ works when men give Him opportunity. But He will not run roughshod over a man's personal sovereignty. He will not force Himself into a man's life against that man's will. He will give healing and peace and salvation only to that man who will meet the conditions, who will receive Christ.

The tragedy is not that Christ has failed or that His church has failed. The tragedy is that men have played at Christianity and church or have rejected it altogether. Obviously it won't work if men won't work it! There's only one way to discover whether medicine works or not. Try it! Argument proves nothing. Debate is fruitless. It has to be applied.

And until a man has tried Christ, until he has met the conditions of repentance and commitment, until a man takes Christ seriously, he is in no position to debate whether Christ works or not. The fact is no man has ever been disappointed in Christ! No man has ever given Him a chance and found Him wanting. Christ has never failed in any test under any conditions—when men have been willing to give Him a chance!

> *If any man chooses to do God's will, he*
> *will find out.*   —John 7:17
> *O taste and see that the Lord is good.*
>   —Psalm 34:8

 Wednesday

Childlikeness! The prerequisite to mature understanding and true wisdom. Not childishness, but childlikeness, the true scientific spirit. Sheer objectivity toward life! "What is that?" the child asks. "That is a chair," answers father. The child has learned something, added to his store of knowledge. He offers no resistance to the instruction. So the child acquires much information and so the inductive process goes on as he learns and grows, accepting the facts as they are given in response to native curiosity.

This is the operation of the scientific method in its purest form. Then comes adolescence, and the child knows so much you can't tell him anything. (The biggest trouble with the adolescent is that he doesn't know what he doesn't know.) He's not wise, just smart. Blissfully unaware of what remains unknown, he thinks he knows everything. The learning process decelerates as resistance to information increases. Native curiosity dwindles as the intellect swells with the minimum of knowledge and experience.

Some adults never pass this stage in spiritual matters. Presuming that competence in other areas of knowledge qualifies them in the realm of the Spirit, they close their minds to the simplest biblical truths. In the name of science they become unscientific, repudiate the inductive process, hold indefensible convictions arrived at by deduction. In the words of Paul, "Although they claimed to be wise, they became fools" (Rom. 1:22). Professing objectivity, the pseudo-intellectual is bound by stubborn, prideful subjectivity. That's adolescence in its most subtle form. It tunes out Jesus

Christ and the Bible without even cursory investigation. Jesus said,

> *I praise you, Father . . . because you have hidden these things from the wise and learned, and revealed them to little children.* —Matthew 11:25

 Thursday

Self is the worst of all tyrants! And no one is more enslaved than he who does as he pleases! Self says, "I do as I please," and calls it freedom, then binds with habits that resist every liberating influence and resolve. A man begins by doing what he wants and finally discovers he is not free to do otherwise. As he pursued his "do-as-I-please" course, his options dwindled; he became less and less able to do as he pleased, more and more limited by the habits cultivated out of the pseudo freedom. Self is an efficient slave master!

Jesus Christ is the greatest of all emancipators! He is able to break the enslaving hold which self lays on one's life. He frees a man to be himself, to fulfill himself, to maximize his potential! He will not impose His will upon a man. He will not violate the personal sovereignty which He guaranteed every man in creation. But when a man consents to the Lordship of Christ, the liberating grace begins to work and leads to exquisite freedom!

Desire to be free? Then seek a master. Seek the Master!

> *So if the Son sets you free, you will be free indeed.* —John 8:36

 Friday

"Peter went outside and wept bitterly." That was the beginning of real manhood for Peter! The manhood was there. It had been built into him at birth, but it needed to be discovered, needed to be released from the false pride under which it was buried. Up to this time Peter was filled with self-sufficiency. He was used to throwing his weight around. The other fishermen respected him and kept their distance. He was strong, outspoken, a born leader, but he needed to be broken. (Like a good horse, a good man needs to be broken before he's really useful.)

A few hours before Peter had boasted to Jesus, "Even if all fall away, I will not." The Lord responded by telling Peter he would deny Him three times before the cock crowed. But Peter boasted more vociferously: "Even if I have to die with you, I will never disown you!" In a matter of hours Peter let the accusation of a little serving girl frighten him into denying Jesus with a curse. "I don't know this man!" Peter blasted profanely. Then the cock crowed. Peter remembered what Jesus had said, and he went out and wept, a broken man!

That was the beginning of true greatness in Peter! Now he began to see himself as God saw him. He began to see his weakness, his pride, his false strength, his bullheadedness, his outspokenness. He was rocked by the realization that he was everything his given name "Simon" implied. Simon means "weak," "fickle," yet Jesus had called him a "rock" (Peter). The thing he needed to learn, however, was that only Jesus can make a Peter out of a Simon. Only Jesus can make a rock out of a fickle, vacillating, boastful man.

True greatness comes by the road of brokenness! No man is really great who has not been broken before God. Until a man comes to the end of himself, until he reaches his extremity and becomes aware of his limitations, until he weeps over his own failure, he may be cocky and loud and bullish, but never great. Peter learned to depend completely on God. He learned that he could be a man only when he humbled himself before God and bowed to the reign and rule of God in his life. The strongest men in the world are those who are weak before God. The greatest men are those who are humble before God. The tallest men are those who bend before God. This is the basic paradox of life: a man's greatness lies in his weakness. When self-sufficiency turns into Christ-confidence, a man is ready for anything!

> *Apart from me you can do nothing.*
> —John 15:5

> *I can do everything through him who gives me strength.* —Philippians 4:13

 Monday

Have you received the forgiveness of God? Then forgive yourself! Don't drag out of the past that which God has forgiven and forgotten. Don't pester your conscience with sin that has been covered by the blood of Christ (atonement means covering). Don't let guilt drain you of your strength like an unhealed wound in the spirit, "pour pus into your bloodstream," or keep you in a state of "spiritual invalidism." If God has forgiven you by virtue of the sacrifice of His Son, no one, including yourself, has a right to condemn you. Paul makes this very clear in a word to the Romans: "Who would dare to accuse us, whom God has chosen? The judge himself has declared us free from sin. Who is in a position to condemn? Only

Christ, and Christ died for us" (Rom. 8:33-34, Phillips).

The Bible abounds in promises of forgiveness for the sinner who confesses his sin and receives God's gracious absolution! "Come now, let us reason together, says the Lord: though your sins be as scarlet, they shall be as white as snow; though they are red like crimson, they shall become like wool" (Isa. 1:18). "As far as the east is from the west, so far does he remove our transgressions from us" (Ps. 103:12). Once sin is confessed, it is forgiven and forgotten by God. He expects us to appropriate His grace and live in His love and forgiveness.

God has forgiven you. Forgive yourself!

> *If we confess our sins, he is faithful and just and will forgive us our sins and purify us from all unrighteousness.*
>
> —1 John 1:9

 Tuesday

Sometime when you find yourself caught in a web of circumstance so thick it is suffocating, or conditions are so bad it seems they could not be worse, or when pressure is so great that you feel you're going to crack up, stop for a moment,

116

shove everything aside, and let yourself relax. Give your mind a chance to breathe. Ask yourself this question: "Ten years from now, or five, or one, or a month from now, how important will the things be that are bothering me now?" One thing that is beating good men to death in this fast-moving, pressure-infested twentieth century is this business of majoring in minors. We get all excited about little things that in a year or a month will not amount to anything at all. But we allow them to mess up the present so much that they are endangering our future. You can shut out the sun with a penny! Just get the penny close enough to your eye. Little things can completely obscure big, important things when you get too close to them. Little things can hem you in, suffocate you, get life all out of proportion.

That's why a perspective is important. You need to step out away from the fussy little things that are so bothersome. Get away from them long enough to see them as they are, in their right proportions.

There's a busy executive who has learned the secret of perspective. Every once in a while, when the pressure gets tense, he clears his cluttered desk and sits quietly for thirty minutes. He sets his heart and mind on God. He reads the Bible, prays, and commits his way to the Lord. He has discovered it dispels the fog from his brain and makes it possible for him to go back to his work renewed, clear-headed, decisive! He's got a cutting edge on his thinking. His insights are sharper. Thirty minutes of quiet before God brings him back to earth and gives him a perspective from which to view his work objectively. Things fall into place in right proportion. He distinguishes between important and unimportant things. First things are done first!

The tragedy of modern living is the number of top men in their middle years who are going to pieces, cracking up, falling apart. The pressures of life are crushing them, rattling their nerves, unsettling them. They are losing their grip, their drive, their incentive. Waiting on God is the antidote, the solution. There's no alternative to quietness. Nothing else settles a man so readily. You're missing a great opportunity when you neglect a quiet time every day—a time for the Bible and prayer!

> *In quietness and in trust shall be your strength.*   —Isaiah 30:15

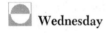 **Wednesday**

Waiting on God is not idleness! Waiting on God is involvement—involvement in the ultimate. Waiting on God is the way to maximum efficiency and effectiveness. The man who refuses to wait on God may be busy—but much of his activity is busy-ness, not business. He may be going places, but he doesn't know where. "Rat race" is not inaccurate in describing his plight.

Waiting on God is not a pious practice; it's a practical rule for life. To wait on God is to have perspective. To wait on God is to be primed, to move productively. The prophet Isaiah put it this way (40:31): "They who wait for the Lord shall renew their strength, they shall mount up with wings like eagles, they shall run and not be weary, they shall walk and not faint."

Waiting on God is the way of renewed strength. Not to wait on God is the way of exhaustion. Waiting on God is to mount up with wings—and stay there. It is to run and not be weary. The man who will not wait wears out prematurely. To wait is to walk and not faint.

No time is wasted waiting on God. Much time will be saved by this practice. Take some time every day, preferably in the morning, to read the Bible and pray and listen. Give God a chance to speak to you, to direct you, to give you a lead on your day. Seek His guidance throughout the day. Engage in "expostulatory prayer," even if all you can say is "Help, God!" Ask God's direction and expect it—you'll not be disappointed. Go with God!

They who wait for the Lord shall renew their strength, they shall mount up with wings like eagles, they shall run and not

be weary, they shall walk and not faint.
                                        —Isaiah 40:31

Thursday

When you can think of nothing to do, that's the thing to do—nothing! Doing something, when one can't think of anything to do, only compounds the problem. Such action is often generated by panic or hysteria. It's the reflex of anxiety, and it usually aborts.

When in difficulty, doing something because one can't think of anything to do will probably deepen the difficulty and add confusion. Look at it this way: Under pressure, when you feel you must do something even though you can't think of what to do, do nothing! That's something! Doing nothing is a strategy—a conscious, positive, constructive strategy.

Leave a glass of muddy water alone and the dirt and debris settle to the bottom; water comes up crystal clear. This is a way of purifying water, and it's a way of allowing a confused situation to clarify. It's the way to approach a problem with a clear head instead of a muddled brain. Waiting is not a waste. On the contrary, it is a wise technique which generates intelligent action.

Waiting brings facts into focus and helps one see them in perspective.

> *He who believes will not be in haste.*
> —Isaiah 28:16
> *They who wait for the Lord shall renew their strength.* —Isaiah 40:31

 Friday

Has God ever spoken to you? Have you ever listened? It is not that God fails to speak, but that we fail to listen. We are so easily distracted; in fact, it rarely if ever occurs to us to listen to God. Distractions are a lame excuse for indifference.

When was the last time you gave God your ear for five minutes? How long has it been since you quietly waited upon God, expecting Him to speak to you? Have you ever done it? "Mystical," "far-fetched," "unreal," "impractical," you say? On what grounds do you dispose of this possibility so easily? What intelligent, rational justification do you have for ignoring the voice of God?

It is hardly intelligent to totally reject something about which you know nothing, something you have never tested and tried! Like rejecting a radio, refusing to listen, before you turn it on and tune it in to a station; or laughing-off television when you have never taken the time to investigate, turn the dial, view a program. Radio and television won't work unless you tune them in. The sound waves are there, the light waves are there, simply waiting the proper connection to bring their message to your ears and eyes. The message is there, but you've got to tune in!

God will speak, is speaking, has spoken, but we've been too busy or too indifferent or too smart to listen. Try it today, right now, before you forget. Take ten minutes to listen to God. You'll be surprised, and grateful. You'll never spend minutes more wisely, more profitably!

Speak, Lord, for thy servant hears.
—1 Samuel 3:9

 Monday

"A reading schedule of only fifteen minutes a day will make it possible for you to complete twenty-five books a year," says a publishing executive. "The science of psychology has made us aware of the fact that in addition to our conscious thought processes, we also have a subconscious mind. This is our data receiving and processing station," he continues. "It does not think or create for itself, and yet it tends to govern our behavior more than our conscious mind. Our sub-conscious mind registers eternally every thought that passes our consciousness. It may be likened to an electronic data computer that accumulates every bit of data that is fed into it and then feeds it back on demand."

Think this through and check your reading habits! Try as you will to impress people with controlled actions, what you really are under-neath, where the subconscious reigns, keeps push-ing through to substantiate or contradict what you are trying to be. "Seventy-five percent of human action is controlled by the unconscious, only 25 percent by the consciousness."[*] "Like an iceberg, only one-eighth of which is above the surface, so is man's personality; seven-eighths of it remains hidden, below the depths of consciousness."[*] "All of our real thinking and three-quarters of our mental activity transpires below the depth of our awareness and only comes to the surface as the time of active use arrives."[*]

The big question is: What are you feeding your subconscious? Do you force upon it a diet of husks: comics, pulp magazines, "sex-satiated slicks and trivia"? Or do you just soak in front of a TV set? Inevitably the payoff will be substandard per-sonality. Nourish your mind with quality reading or your character is fighting a losing battle. Feed

[*]Charles Mayo
[*]G. Stanley Hall
[*]David Seabury

your soul on garbage and you cultivate a pig's outlook.

> *The good man brings good things out of the good stored up in him, and the evil man brings evil things out of the evil stored up in him.* —Matthew 12:35

 Tuesday

Looks can be deceiving in watches and in men.

You learn about watches in Hong Kong. If you're not an expert, be sure you visit a reliable dealer, or you may be sold a watch with a beautiful case and an attractive face; it may even have the label of a well-known Swiss company. Then you discover the works are cheap. It's what's inside that counts!

So with man. He may be the picture of sartorial excellence, maintain a smiling and gracious countenance, speak winsome and compelling words. But what's inside? That's the clue to the man.

Sooner or later, what he is on the inside shows through. Looks and rhetoric and posture do not reveal the Christian. A heart of love for God and man does! "I really trusted that watch," said the man as he missed the train. "Faith without works is dead," replied a friend.

Man looks on the outward appearance, but the Lord looks on the heart.
—1 Samuel 16:7

 Wednesday

The man insists on the finest steak cooked to perfection—and he reads *Playboy!* He nourishes his stomach on the best food money can buy and feeds his mind on photos of nude women and a philosophy of life that panders sex to its panting clientele. Pitiful what some men give their minds to chew on. They demand the best food for their bodies and stuff their intellects with garbage.

No wonder their hearts are starved: bodies fat and well-fed, intellects and emotions suffering malnutrition. The more greedily, breathlessly, he devours husks, the more his heart languishes for solid food. And out of the heart come the issues of life.

Frightening, when you stop to think what some decision makers are nurturing their imaginations on. What is the raw material of their policy? Where do they get the ideas that flourish and fructify in their brains? What do their emotions feed on as they wrestle with big issues? What stimulates their imaginations as they confront the ponderous problems that beset our contemporary world? Come to think of it, moral and ethical decline is no mystery in the light of the reading matter being consumed by some of our "best minds." The plain fact is that we get out what we put in!

> *The good man brings good things out of the good stored up in him, and the evil man brings evil things out of the evil stored up in him.* —Matthew 12:35

 Thursday

Some people never have accidents; they just cause them! They drive down the highway as though they were walking a tightrope, so pre-occupied with safety that they constitute a hazard to normal traffic. Priding themselves on their "safety" record, they are utterly oblivious to the accidents or near-accidents caused by their fears. Overcautious, they hunt and pick their way through traffic as though they were walking on eggs, or they cling to a position on the road, usually hard to center, as though afraid they were going to fall off. Meanwhile traffic backs up and pressure builds up dangerously behind these bottlenecks of caution.

Likewise, some men with pea-picking piety manage to avoid trouble, but they are continually making it for others. Walking the "straight and narrow" they maintain a meticulous posture of piety (they think), while the censure and criticism they peddle blackens others. With consummate delusion, these self-appointed judges, like semi-professional providences, feel they are doing God a favor. Carefully avoiding every outward appearance of evil, their hearts are filled with vitriol which their tongues spit out continually. These self-styled amateur critics gloat in their facade of righteousness, when inwardly they are a cauldron of vicious, malicious bitterness. In devious and subtle ways they spew out their acid, unmoved by the scorched lives withered in the blast.

What a sordid contrast to the kindness and tenderness and compassion of Jesus. How unlike their blessed Lord of love these pious phonies are!

> *Woe to you, teachers of the law and Pharisees, you hypocrites! For you are like whitewashed tombs, which look beautiful on the outside but on the inside are full of dead men's bones and everything unclean. In the same way, on the outside you appear to people as righteous but on the inside you are full of hypocrisy and wickedness. You snakes!*

You brood of vipers! How will you escape being condemned to hell?
                              —Matthew 23:27-28, 33

Friday

Why work? Why go to college? Youth are asking such questions today, not because they are lazy (though many are), but because they have been given the wrong reasons for work, for getting a college education. They have been taught to believe that one works to make money; the harder one works, the more money one makes. Or one goes to college and gets a degree because the degree guarantees a better job with a bigger salary and prestige.

Unfortunately, the adults who have been attempting to motivate youth with this argument often fail to demonstrate any real benefits in their own lives. They have a college education, but they are not happy. They work hard, earn plenty of money, but there's no love in their home. The money which they held up as motivation for work or college has not produced desirable results in their lives. They haven't convinced youth that their values are worth striving for.

One young man who copped out went the drug route, ended up in Washington, D.C., and was led to Christ by some young street workers who took him to a farm in Pennsylvania for rehabilitation. He worked: preparing soil, seeding, weeding, etc. Finally the day came when he ate the food which he had produced and discovered the real reason for work—to produce! He was thrilled with the result of his own labor and realized for the first time the authentic benefit of it.

> *So God created man in His image.... God blessed them; God said to them: Be fruitful; multiply; fill the earth and subdue it.* —Genesis 1:27-28
> (*Modern Language Bible*)

 Monday

Sure we believe in the freedom of speech. Each person has the right to say what he thinks. He can even libel another if he cares to take the risk. He's got the right to say anything he likes. But no one has to listen! People have as much right not to listen as one has to say what he pleases. They can "tune him out" any time they wish—they are under no obligation to "tune him in." Our right to speak is guaranteed; but we must earn the right to be listened to!

The right to be heard depends solely upon the integrity of the speaker, not upon any obligation of the listener. Talk away on the ground of your rights, but by the same token, allow the other man his right not to listen. The right to be heard depends upon responsibility! It may be a much-worn cliche, "Your actions speak so loud that I cannot hear what you say," but it's never been more relevant.

Our modern world, conditioned by the empirical approach to life, jaded by the daily massive assault of mass communication, is more pragmatic than ever. Demonstrable proof is prerequisite to acceptance in contemporary life. Responsibility of action is an intelligent and compelling corollary to the right to speak. If you expect to be listened to, back your words up with your life! That's fundamental to Christian witness in the twentieth century!

> *Why do you call me 'Lord, Lord,' and do not do what I say?* —Luke 6:46

 Tuesday

Democracy doesn't work without the Bible! We take its roots for granted and assume democracy will work anywhere like it works in America. We are frustrated by its failure in emerging independent nations, perplexed by the ease with which dictatorships or autocracies take over. We suffer the illusion that "self-determination" is a passion with people everywhere, when in reality nothing could be further from the truth. The fact is, the concept of self-determination is a product of the Judeo-Christian tradition received from the Bible.

Our Western world has been immersed in this tradition for centuries. In the words of a leading American, it is "in our bloodstream." "We hold these truths to be self-evident; that all men are created equal; and that they are endowed by their creator with certain unalienable rights." That was the deepest conviction of the founders of the oldest democratic republic in the world, and they engraved it on the cornerstone of America. The very heart and soul of democracy is the inherent dignity of man and the supreme worth of the individual. That's an exclusively biblical concept! It is foreign to non-biblical cultures. They may try to copy democracy, imitate what the West has been doing for centuries, but it simply doesn't work. They have the theory without the substance. They get the idea, but there's no heart in it. The experiment collapses on the concept of man. "What is man?" Human value and dignity eludes them. Concern for the "common good" is as rare as snow in July in cultures where the Judeo-Christian tradition has had relatively little impact.

Legislation cannot dismiss in a generation what

by their creator with certain unalienable rights." Those majestic words engraved on the cornerstone of America beg to be thoughtfully considered at this moment in our history. They speak truths which are indisputable.

They speak of belief in a Creator which is the ground of human dignity and worth. No Creator, no equality! No Creator, no unalienable rights! Rejection of the Creator has destructive consequences for our republic.

Equally destructive are those who profess belief in the Creator and ignore or repudiate the "self-evident" truths which are implicit in that belief. Their professed piety does not abrogate their guilt in denying by their attitudes and practices the equality of all men. Their failure or refusal to recognize that all men have "certain unalienable rights" is a denial of the spirit of America, all their claims of patriotism to the contrary notwithstanding.

As we approach the 200th birthday of our nation, let each ask himself whether or not he really believes in America and the basic principles which make her great. Let each examine his life style as to whether or not it corresponds to those principles. "We hold these truths to be self-evident; that all men are created equal; and that they are endowed by their creator with certain unalienable rights." "In God we trust."

For from him (God) and through him and

to him are all things. To him be the glory
forever! Amen. —Romans 11:36

Thursday

There is a God-given formula for peace and healing in our land. Until we've taken this seriously, we're shutting the door to fundamental improvement. The most significant thing about this formula for national peace and prosperity is that it is addressed to the people of God, those who are called by God's name. The people of God are the key to the situation. They always have been and always will be. Because this nation had its birth in biblical faith! Its major documents, its founding struggles were saturated with prayer and earnest seeking for God's will and way. This is where indictment for our national waywardness begins! Not with the atheists. Not with the pagans. Not with unbelievers and infidels. But with the people of God!

It is foolish to say there is no God. But it is infinitely more foolish to say there is and to live as though there were not. This kind of practical atheism is the crux of our trouble in America! The multiplied millions of good, intelligent, responsible men and women who believe in God, who received a rich spiritual heritage from their parents, but who now disregard God for all practical purposes—these are the root of our need. This is secularism in its worst form. This is the place where judgment must begin—at the house of God. Like an insidious, malignant disease, this practical godlessness is eating away at the vital center of American life. Communism and corruption simply cannot take root in a society where men and women believe in God and take that belief seriously enough to live as though they do. Materialism and secularism are fertile soil for infections like Communism.

God does not withdraw His blessing from a nation without provocation! God is "slow to anger," "plenteous in mercy," but He cannot bless a people who reject Him and His blessing in practice, if not in theory. Four conditions we must meet: humble ourselves, pray, seek God's face, and turn from our wicked ways. If we meet these conditions, God has promised to do something for our nation. But not until! These four conditions fall under one heading—repentance! This is the real need among the people of God. This is where national blessing and healing begins.

> *If my people who are called by my name humble themselves, and pray and seek my face, and turn from their wicked ways, then I will hear from heaven, and will forgive their sin and heal their land.*
> —2 Chronicles 7:14

Men who fear men more than fear God! Men in high places who profess to be Christian but are unwilling to talk publicly about Jesus Christ. In their fear of offending men they are silent about Christ. In so doing, they offend Christ. In offending Christ, they offend God and neutralize the Christian witness. Are they leaders who capitulate again and again to a profane society and refuse to take a bold stand for Christian conviction, who submit meekly as men degrade the name of Jesus in profanity, drag that dear name into the gutter with all manner of foul language and smut, while they studiously avoid any reference to Jesus in their conversation?

What a contradiction! Ungodly men unafraid and unashamed to desecrate the name of Jesus anywhere, anytime; while men who profess devotion to Him dare not mention His name. How easily men in public life justify their silence, their fear, their compromise: "I can't talk about Christ. There may be a Jew present and I would not want to offend him." It is not the Christian's devotion to Jesus that offends the Jew; it is the inconsistent, un-Christlike attitude toward Jews on the part of some who profess Christ. It is not the use of Jesus' name which offends; it is the utterly unchristian spirit of anti-Semitism practiced by some so-called Christians. (I have never met a does with them, that makes the difference! Most things in this life are either a blessing or a curse depending on the use to which man puts them! This is the key to the solution of every problem!

Take for example the technological progress man has made in the past twenty years. Never in history has man's know-how been so finely developed. Yet man uses his gadgets and gimmicks selfishly, destructively, and turns a blessing into a curse. It's the same with science. Scientific research and production have made immeasurable advances. Yet today the fruit of science is what man fears most. Not because it is bad in itself, but because of the possibilities of man's use of it. Money is a blessing or a curse depending on how a man uses it. As long as a man possesses his money and uses it wisely, it's a blessing to his life. But the minute money begins to possess the man, dictate to him, it is devastating! Pleasure is a blessing or a curse. Some men live for pleasure, let it run and ruin their lives. Other men take pleasure as it comes, as a by-product of life, one of the incidental returns of a life well lived. Then pleasure is constructive, edifying, productive—a blessing!

Even virtue can be a blessing or a curse! Let a man boast of his virtue, pride himself on his achievement morally and he is drawn inevitably into self-righteous pharisaism. Virtue becomes a vice. Humility is a virtue. But let a man be self-conscious of his humility and he turns it into pride; let him talk about his humility and he turns it into arrogance. Humility talked about is humility degenerated into conceit!

Jesus Christ Himself is a blessing or a curse depending on what a man does with Him! He is either a man's Savior or a man's Judge. He either commends a man to God or, if a man rejects Christ, condemns him; the man stands condemned by his rejection! This is perfectly illustrated by the two thieves who hung on either side of Christ at His crucifixion. One appealed to Christ and asked for mercy. It was granted. The other rebelled, rejected Him, and went out under his own condemnation. Condemned by refusing the love that would redeem him!

> *Whoever believes in him is not condemned, but whoever does not believe stands condemned already because he has not believed in the name of God's one and only Son.* —John 3:18

 Tuesday

They call it "universalism." The belief that all will finally be saved—that no one will perish because of sin. In other words, there is no fear of hell. Generally this doctrine's final appeal is to the justice of God, the implication being that a just and loving God would not ultimately reject anyone. Which is true. God will not—does not—reject anyone!

But the problem is not God's rejection of man; it is man's rejection of God. God loves the world and everyone in it through history. His love is universal and all-inclusive, a perfect love in which God sent His only Son to die on the cross for all in every generation from the first to the last.

But God cannot force anyone to accept that love! That would not be love but coercion, which denies the freedom God guaranteed to man in creation. (Rejection of creation repudiates that freedom.) God created man free—free even to reject God: His will, His order, His salvation, and His love. Sin is disbelief and rejection. To reject God's truth and love is the profoundest of sins —the fundamental sin of history.

Salvation is universal. Christ died for all and desires that all enjoy heaven. But the stubborn fact is that not all believe and accept His love and His salvation. Many—perhaps most—reject it. God has not rejected them; they have rejected Him!

> *This is the verdict: Light has come into the world, but men loved darkness instead of light because their deeds were evil.*　　　　　　　—John 3:19

Government by law or by man, those are the alternatives. Government by man leads inevitably to tyranny or anarchy. Anarchy, by its very nature, encourages and abets the rise to leadership of the strong man; hence tyranny is bred of anarchy. The best that government by man can offer is a benevolent despot. Human nature being what it is, with its susceptibility to the corruptible influence of power, benevolent despotism is a rather vain hope.

Assuming sincerity on the part of a minority of revolutionary youth, whose revulsion against the materialism of their elders is expressed in various kinds of revolt, their delusion, apart from their tragic and naive capitulation to subversive conspiracy against the U.S.A., is their failure to recognize that government by law is the only guarantee of the justice they espouse. To equate contemporary violence with the American Revolution is like comparing gangsterism with a legislative process. Whatever else was involved in the American Revolution, it was a repudiation of tyranny and the adoption of government by law. Respect for law and order was its fundamental spirit. Responsibility, individual and corporate, was the keystone.

Personal integrity and honor were the hallmarks of the revolutionaries. Their objectives were constructive and positive. These qualities were born in the hearts of men who held a deep and abiding sense of accountability to God and to man. Which gives us the clue that it was, above everything, spiritual at its roots. "We hold these truths to be self-evident; that all men are created equal; that they are endowed by their creator with certain unalienable rights . . . that to secure these rights, governments are instituted among men."

> *For there is no authority except that which God has established.*
> —Romans 13:1

 Thursday

A bishop of the Lutheran Church in India visited with the prime minister of an Asian country at the time the World Council of Churches met in Evanston, Illinois. The theme of the World Council meeting was "Jesus Christ the Hope of the World."

"That theme is very presumptuous," declared the prime minister.

"Do you not believe it is true?" queried the bishop.

"No!" answered the minister. "Buddhism is the

hope of the world. Buddhism has not bathed the world in blood as Christianity has."

There's no easy answer to such an indictment: Two world wars in a quarter century, precipitated by a "Christian nation," the matrix of much of modern Christian theology; a "Christian nation" first to use the atom bomb with its incalculable destruction and misery to two Asian cities. ("Are you a Christian?" the American asked a Japanese girl, his guide in Hiroshima. "I used to be," she replied, "but not any more; now I'm Buddhist." "Have you changed because of what happened here?" he asked. "Yes!")

If you were an African, and a Moslem urged you to embrace Islam on the grounds of the way "Christian America" treats the Negro, what would you do? What is the explanation for these terrible contradictions? One significant clue is the perennial effort that is made to change society without benefit of the Gospel of Christ. That's like trying to stop the decay of a corpse with an ideology. We have been resolving and educating and pontificating and negotiating and socializing and lobbying and legislating ad-infinitum; but we haven't been preaching the Gospel! In the interest of modernity and liberalism we have neglected or abandoned the only force in history which can subdue the passion of men and nations. We have emasculated the only power on earth which can stay the corruption of society. Involved with institutionalism, intellectualism, and internationalism, we have failed to witness to the Gospel of the love of God in Christ's death and resurrection. Preoccupied with man's temporal need, we have forfeited his eternal welfare. Forfeiting man's eternal welfare, we have defaulted in his present predicament. The pay-off: a "form of godliness without the power," nominal Christianity which is in fact secularized paganism, a reproach to Christ and His gospel. Jesus said,

> *Isaiah was right when he prophesied about you hypocrites; as it is written: These people honor me with their lips, but their hearts are far from me. They worship me in vain; their teachings are but rules made by men.* —Mark 7:6-7

 Friday

"Economic determinism!" One of the fundamentals of Communism: the principle that life is determined, not by spiritual, but by economic forces. Christians reject this principle in theory, but what about practice?

How many of us are regimented by the culture of our day? By status and position and prestige? By cars and clothes and houses? Think how our lives are influenced by economic forces. We invest the best we have to offer in the race for acquisition. We strive and struggle and sacrifice for economic goals. Almost our total preoccupation is with life this side of the grave. Emphasis is on the tangible, the temporal, the transitory. We are hooked by affluence! We are the slaves of economic forces! Our hang-up is the status quo! We oppose Communism while at the same time we capitulate to one of its fundamental dynamics.

The power of faith is in its authentic other-worldliness. Jesus incarnated it, demonstrated it, demanded it!

> *No one can serve two masters. Either he will hate the one and love the other, or he will be devoted to the one and despise the other. You cannot serve God and Money.... But seek first his kingdom and his righteousness.* —Matthew 6:24, 33

 Monday

World Vision Magazine (April-May 1972) carried the following description of a microcosm of our world. It's provocative and soul-searching.

"Let our world of 3.5 billion persons be represented by a small town of 3500. And let our small town be a miniature of our world today. Its population has increased 50 percent in only 30 years.

"In our town of 3500: 200 of us live high on a hill (called the developed countries), overlooking the town, and 3300 are on the rocky bottomland called the rest of the world. The fortunate 200 have over 50 percent of the wealth of the whole town and over half of all the rooms in the town with two rooms per person. The 3300 people have less than half of all the rooms with five persons to a room. According to the best estimates, the people on the hill have: 80 percent of all the bath tubs of the whole town, 75 percent of all the radios and TV sets, 50 percent of all the telephones, and an average income per person of $3159 per year. The rest of the town gets an average of about $200 per year per person, most of them only $100 or less.

"How does this fortunate group use its incredible wealth? Well, per family it spends: $850 per year to protect itself from some of the other people in the town, $83.50 on gambling, $55.50 on alcoholic beverages, and $33.30 on instant lung cancer, but $1.63 per year per person to share its knowledge of Jesus Christ with the rest of the town. The 200 on the hill also have 90 percent of all the ministers in the town."

From everyone who has been given much, much will be demanded.

—Luke 12:48

Two things you need, I need, every man needs! To be known and to belong. Being known is more basic than knowing. Belonging more important than having. The soul of man hungers and thirsts most deeply to be known and to belong.

Spiritual homesickness is his deepest alienation. "Nobody understands me!" That is the cry of the bitterest loneliness experienced by man. It is at the heart of adolescent frustration, the root of deepest insecurity. And man never gets over this need.

Hence the extraordinary measures taken by intelligent adults to gain the acceptance of their peers and the intense suffering experienced when they are rejected. Ultimate resolution is in the love of God! He knows you like an open book; your future is as plain to Him as your past. You have no secrets from Him; He knows you better than you know yourself—infinitely better. Realize this and you're home!

> *O Lord, thou hast searched me and known me! Thou knowest when I sit down and when I rise up; thou discernest my thoughts from afar.... Even before a word is on my tongue, lo, O Lord, thou knowest it altogether.*
> —Psalm 139:1, 4 (Read it all.)

There is at least one thing worse than having a disease, and that's to have a disease and not know it! Like a friend of years past. He ignored pains in his abdomen for years, refusing to see the doctor. He was tough, and proud! Until the pain became unbearable and he had to see the doctor, who ordered surgery and discovered the abdominal region was filled with cancer. He didn't even try to take it out—just sewed him up. My friend died a few days later.

Almost daily I meet tough, proud men who refuse to admit they are sinners. They stay away from church because the preacher talks about sin; they refuse to read the Bible for the same reason. Incurably humanistic, they refuse to believe anything but the best about man in general, themselves in particular. Despite all the evidence of history to the contrary. Despite all contemporary evidence of man's violence, bigotry, pride, selfishness, hate, greed, and avarice. Despite the Bible's insistence that "All have sinned and fall short of the glory of God. There is no one righteous, not even one" (Rom. 3:23, 10).

The wise man discovers cancer in its early stages and allows medical science to deal with it. The wise man accepts the Bible's diagnosis of his sinful condition, believes the Bible's remedy, and receives the cure through Jesus Christ and the Gospel. Jesus said,

> *(The world hates) me because I testify*
> *that what it does is evil.*   —John 7:7
> *The blood of Jesus, his Son, purifies us*
> *from every sin.*   —1 John 1:7

 Thursday

A friend writes: "I guess I have a typical case of I believe but I doubt. I doubt that God is guiding me regarding my future. For the past five years my job history has been quite poor, not by my choice, but by circumstances I had little to do with. No doubt my faith has grown with these experiences, but when does it stop? Naturally I want some security with a happy job, but when does this, if ever, come about? I'm grateful for health, family, etc., but boy, does it get frustrating regarding this employment thing."

What does one do in such a situation? He begins by accepting the fact of his circumstances as they are. One of the hardest things we have to do is accept things as they are, but that is the only solid foundation for growth and progress. We keep trying to build on things as we wish they were. That's like starting to build from the top down. The dreams keep collapsing. You cannot begin where you are not!

Wherever you are, however difficult it is, however adverse the circumstances, that's where you must begin. That's where God's will begins. The Apostle Paul knew the secret. He wrote, "I have learned to be content whatever the circumstances" (Phil. 4:10). He wrote, "... by the grace of God I am what I am" (1 Cor. 15:10). He didn't resign himself to the status quo, nor did he resent reversals. He rejoiced in whatever his circumstances were in the conviction that God was leading. Favorable circumstances do not necessarily indicate divine favor, nor do unfavorable circumstances indicate divine displeasure. God's promise to lead, despite the circumstances, is all we need. That's the way of faith!

> *And we know that in all things God works for the good of those who love him, who have been called according to his purpose.* —Romans 8:28

 Friday

Truth is always exclusive! You cannot make a true statement about anything without excluding others, whatever area of life is being discussed.

Two plus two equals four. That excludes three or five. The shortest distance between two points is a straight line. Crooked lines need not apply. Men are operating on this basis all the time: stating truths which in the nature of things exclude other views.

Error is a fact of life too, and truth and error are mutually exclusive. Yet there are those offended by Jesus' statement, "I am the way—and the truth and the life. No one comes to the Father except through me" (John 14:6). If Jesus is not the only way to the Father, how many other ways are there? Or are all ways to the Father true ways? If not, who decided which are the true ways and which are not? How bad (or wrong) does a man have to be to miss the way; or how good (or right) does a man have to be to make it? Who decides where the line is drawn between making and missing the way? Unless you insist that any way is right and true, you eliminate some, and the minute you eliminate some, you are the judge of which ways are to be excluded. You are guilty of the same narrowness of which you accuse Jesus.

It is just possible that in an effort to broaden the way to God you actually make it more exclusive than Jesus does. In fact, think it through and see if you can come up with a way less exclusive than Jesus' invitation, "Whosoever will may come." One can hardly issue a more generous invitation than that. If some condition more than willingness is required, what is that condition to

a thing about it. In a word, it's indifference—that is robbing us of everything that is important and different about our nation. Indifference and apathy are our worst enemies. Millions of Americans are indifferent to who's elected president. They're indifferent to foreign policy, local politics, management and labor problems. They're indifferent to public and civic projects: Red Cross, Community Chest, Y.M.C.A. All these and many others pass by and they remain totally and smugly unmoved. Inert!

The horizon of their interest is self. They are little people all bottled up in themselves. Little countries bounded on the north, south, east, and west by self.

> "I had a little tea-party,
> This afternoon at three;
> 'Twas very small,
> Three guests in all,
> Just I, myself, and me.
> Myself ate up the sandwiches,
> While I drank up the tea,
> 'Twas also I
> Who ate the pie
> And passed the cake to me."*

We must awaken, shake ourselves out of this indifferent slump, and alert ourselves to basic issues. We must return to the foundation of America: faith in God and obedience to His Word.

*From *Three Guests* by Jessica Nelson North

Democracy is not a root; it's a branch, of which Christianity is the root. At least we ought to take the trouble to investigate the real conditions that are to be met to have the America our forefathers intended! "Men must be governed by God, or they will be ruled by tyrants."*

> *But seek first his kingdom and his righteousness, and all these things will be given to you as well.* —Matthew 6:33

*William Penn

 Tuesday

Do you have a personal history with Jesus Christ? Or is your faith secondhand? One man says, "Of course I'm a Christian. I was born in America." Another says, "Sure I'm a Christian. I'm not a Jew;" or "Do you think I'm a heathen (by which he means a jungle native or an illiterate aboriginal)? Of course I'm a Christian!" Someone else says, "My father was a preacher (or a deacon, or an usher, or a Sunday school teacher)." Some boast of a great ancestry in the church.

But you can't inherit Christianity! It comes firsthand! In fact, the man who enjoys a rich Christian heritage is so much the more condemned if he has not been induced by such a legacy to personal commitment to Christ. (Knowledge equals responsibility.) Resting on the laurels of past generations, a man damns his own soul. The greater his opportunity to embrace authentic Christianity, the greater his judgment if he neglects it. Christian faith involves a firsthand experience of Jesus Christ Himself. The Christian enjoys a personal, living relationship with the Son of God.

History is basic to Christian faith, but it is more than history. Christ is contemporary! He did not remain in the tomb; He rose from the grave. He has confronted every subsequent generation as the living Lord! How a man responds to Christ today is the most vital issue in life: the eternal welfare of his soul, his present, personal effectiveness here and now, depend upon this relationship. Christ confronts each man today through His church, its worship, the Scriptures, the sermon, Christian fellowship, the witness of individual Christians, and the circumstances of life. Christ confronts each man, seeking his trust and obedience, seeking to give him all that God has offered for time and eternity. What will you do with Jesus? What is He to you? What place do you give Him in your life?

Whoever believes in him is not condemned, but whoever does not believe stands condemned already because he has not believed in the name of God's one and only Son. —John 3:18

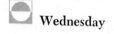

Heaven? How impractical can you get! You believe heaven is irrelevant? Then you have no faith in the future? Why go to high school, college, and graduate school just to get a graduate degree? Why save for a rainy day? Why work your heart out in anticipation of the day of security and retirement?

There's no future so absolutely certain as heaven. There are hundreds of exigencies between now and the degree, now and the rainy day, now and possible retirement. For one thing, you may die or be killed. That won't keep you from heaven, but it may cancel any other future plans you have. Some people reject the idea of heaven and believe in some other utopian dream which has absolutely no guarantee of fulfillment. They criticize faith in heaven as an "opiate" and promote some fanciful, faraway, man-invented utopia which hasn't a ghost of a chance. It leads to nowhere; which is what utopia means.

God invites all to heaven's certainty. He sent His Son who died on the cross to guarantee it! Heaven can't miss. It's got Almighty God behind it, and Jesus Christ is the way to all who accept His love and receive from Him the gift of eternal life.

For God so loved the world that he gave

his one and only Son, that whoever be-
lieves in him shall not perish but have
everlasting life. —John 3:16

 Thursday

Hell? Of course, I believe in it! Moral freedom requires it. Without an alternative to heaven there is no option, no freedom. What kind of God would force men who don't want to, to live in heaven? What meaning would heaven have for those who desire a different way of life? It would be unfair of God not to make a place for those who refuse the kingdom of God; unfair not to allow those who reject the divine order to have their own way.

For those for whom freedom means having their own way, God has made hell! God does not send men to hell; they choose it. God has done all in His power to keep men from hell. He put His Son on a cross. A man has to squeeze past the cross to get into hell. Hell is the alternative to the way of God, the order of God. Hell is the moral alternative to heaven.

The Lord ... is patient with you, not
wanting anyone to perish. —2 Peter 3:9
For God so loved the world that he gave

his one and only Son, that whoever be-
lieves in him shall not perish but have
everlasting life. —John 3:16

 Friday

Do you have faith in God or faith in your ideas
about Him? Is God real or just an intellectual
concept? Is He personal or academic? Is He a
living reality in your life or just a theological
proposition? How big is your God? Is He limited
to your understanding, your intellectual grasp,
your rational explanations?

Your God is too small if He is no larger than
your ideas about Him! You are, in fact, creating
your god and he is no god at all, but an idol, a
logical (more or less) syllogism, the product of
your own intellect. Which means that you are
bigger than your god as the creator is greater
than his creature. You are the creator; your god
is your creature. No wonder you have no respect
for your god! No wonder you do not expect anything from him. No wonder life is inside out and
upside down. No wonder your values are trans-
posed and you don't really know what you are
living for. No wonder your religion has form
without power. Half-hearted faith is inevitable
when men downgrade God to their size. If you're

living in a spiritual vacuum, don't be surprised when life seems hollow. If you've got a capital Zero where God ought to be, you're worshiping Nothing!

Want to get squared away? Get your eyes off yourself, your ingenuity, your intellectualism; take a long, clear, honest look at Jesus Christ. Ask Jesus to make Himself known to you. He will make God real to you if you let Him! "For although they knew God, they neither glorified him as God nor gave thanks to him, but thinking became futile and their foolish hearts were darkened. Although they claimed to be wise, they became fools" (Rom. 1:21-22).

> *Jesus answered, "I am the way—and the truth and the life. No one comes to the Father except through me. If you really knew me, you would know my Father as well. From now on, you do know him and have seen him.* —John 14:6-7

 Monday

Let's have some plain talk about this matter of profanity! Let's talk squarely, open-mindedly, honestly about it. We need to, for it's so tragically common among men—a terrible indictment against us. Profanity can be damaging! As for example an experience at a service club lunch with a friend. It was an important occasion with many prominent men present. A number of the club leaders were introduced, men who had contributed a great deal by way of service. The speaker, international president on his annual visitation, brought a stirring, thought-provoking address. There was much of Christian idealism in his speech. He urged upon his colleagues the need for a return to the Christian way, Christian home, Christian ideals. It was really an excellent address from beginning to end, and it touched, challenged, and inspired us.

But one of the "wheels" who had been introduced had a part in the program. He punctuated his remarks with "God this," and "God that," using the name of God profanely several times. As we drove back to the office my friend asked: "What's the purpose of that club anyway? The speaker talked about Christian principles and one of the leaders kept using profanity. What's the deal anyway?" My friend wondered if the club really meant what it said. And rightly so. That excellent address, given right from the speaker's heart, was spoiled for my friend because God's name was bandied about by someone—loosely, carelessly.

There's no justification whatever for a Christian man to do this. The Bible is very clear about it. One tenth of the basic moral law of the universe deals with it: "Thou shalt not take the name of the Lord thy God in vain!" Jesus Christ spoke out against it, commanding His disciples never to swear either by heaven or earth. Using God's name in profanity is inexcusable, yet it is done constantly. It's an ugly habit. And to make matters worse, men say they do it unconsciously. In other words they think so little of God that they can use His holy name carelessly, profanely, without even realizing it! Profanity is a weak substitute for good English. It is never right, and it never does any good, either to speaker or hearer. It lowers the whole level of conversation. But most of all, it is a slap in the face to God!

> *Do not swear at all; either by heaven, for it is God's throne; or by the earth, for it is his footstool. . . . anything beyond this comes from the evil one!*
> —Matthew 5:34, 37

 Tuesday

It is not enough just to be against or to be neutral—what are you for? If you refuse the Christian way, what are your alternatives? You will not believe in Christ; in whom then will you believe? You will not come to Christ; to whom will you go? You will not follow Christ; who will you follow?

You believe something even if you insist that you don't believe in anything. Believing in nothing is something! You are following someone, even if you insist you are following nobody. You are living for something, even if you're so busy making a living that you do not know what you are living for. You are going somewhere, even if you have not bothered to get your direction or decide on your destination. You are becoming someone, even though you may be so completely preoccupied with the present that you ignore the future. You've got a destiny, one way or the other, even though you are indifferent to it.

What are the alternatives if you will not have Christ, follow Christ, be Christ's, take Christ's way? Honestly, do you know a better, more intelligent, more honorable and fulfilling way? You're on your way. Why not make it *The Way?* (John 14:6). Jesus said,

> *He who is not with me is against me.*
> —Matthew 12:30

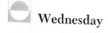 **Wednesday**

Have you been twice born? Jesus said a man must be; He said that entrance into the kingdom of heaven required second birth, a new birth.

In fact He was quite blunt in declaring that one could not even see the kingdom unless he was born anew, a condition laid down to a man highly qualified ethically and religiously—Nicodemus, a ruler of the Jews. Nicodemus was no slouch when it came to religion or morals. He was a good man, an exceedingly good man who took his religion seriously. He was a leader of men, outstanding among his people. Everything about Nicodemus was exemplary. He was a solid citizen, way above the average in the basics of life. But Jesus told him that he lacked that which made possible his entrance into the kingdom of God. His morals and ethics, his civic leadership, his unimpeachable life, his religious sincerity were not adequate; he required the new birth. It takes something more than ethics or religion to get a man into the kingdom!

A Christian is a twice-born man! He is more than a man striving to live a good life, more than a man doing his best! He is the recipient of the gift of God which is eternal life. He is a man in whom the power of God has done that which only God can do—create! He is one who has been made a new man in Christ, literally the product of the creative work of God! Ethics are involved in this work of God, but they are the result of something far more basic—spirituality.

The Christian lives by a new dimension altogether, which was absent from his life until he was regenerated (born anew) by the power of

God. This new dimension (vertical and spiritual) is the root of which true ethics and true morality are the fruit. Christian morality has to do with a man's being rather than his doing, with his nature rather than his deeds. The Christian has a new disposition, a new nature, literally infused into him by the creative act of God through Jesus Christ. Are you a twice-born man? A spiritual man? Or just a natural man doing his best?

You must be born again!   —John 3:7

 Thursday

I believe that the most irrational fact in history is man's rejection of Jesus Christ. It is contrary to all the evidence, unsupportable on any reasonable grounds and indefensible intellectually! Take Jesus' hometown folks for example: The record says that they were astonished at His wisdom and miraculous powers. Yet they "took offense at him."

They reasoned this way: "He is a carpenter, the son of the widow Mary. We know His brothers and sisters." Despite their amazement at His wisdom and His mighty works, they rejected Him! The evidence was overwhelming, but it was immaterial to them. They yielded to their prejudice and deprived themselves of the blessing He could have brought them. "He did not do many miracles there because of their lack of faith" (Matt. 13:58).

Not that His power was any less; they simply would not allow Him to bless them, would not consent to His love. That's unbelief in its naked form. It is not intellectual; it is visceral, volitional. It is not a matter of the head but of the heart. Jesus was a man. That is undeniable. His word and works are a matter of trustworthy record. But once He is accepted as a man, He cannot be explained on merely human terms. One must follow Him or reject Him!

> *But this is the verdict: Light has come into the world, but men loved darkness instead of light because their deeds were evil.* —John 3:19

 Friday

Christianity begins with a changed man! It doesn't end there, but it begins there. The change may be gradual as in the case of Peter who followed Christ and learned of Him during the course of three years; or it may be sudden, as in the case of Paul who was confronted by Christ and changed radically and instantly at the time of his greatest hostility to Christ. Paul's conversion was no more valid or relevant than Peter's; but the point is, they were both converted!

Christianity that does not involve conversion is not Christianity in the New Testament sense. The Christian ethic is the product of Christian faith, not the essence. The essence is a life-changing experience of Jesus Christ! Herein lies the serious weakness of Western Christian culture. It equates Christian ethics with Christianity. It assumes that one who professes the ethic has embraced the faith. It accepts Christ's teachings and rejects Christ Himself. It has the form but lacks the power. The Gospel of Jesus Christ is "the power of God for ... salvation" because it is the power of God to change a man and to produce the righteousness of God in his life.

> *To all who received him (Christ) ... he*
> *gave the right to become children of God.*
> —John 1:12

 Monday

One of the deepest questions perplexing contemporary man is that of authority. What is the ultimate ground of truth? Where does one turn for the court of final appeal, the absolute criterion for truth? Or is there any? Is everything relative? Is there no objective, authoritative, final test?

Ultimately you believe yourself or someone else. You believe what you think and say and write, or you believe what somebody else thinks and says and writes. Wherever you begin, whatever the ground of your convictions, faith is involved—faith in yourself or faith in another.

Furthermore, you decide who or what you are going to trust as the foundation of your life. Choice is inescapable! Consciously, deliberately, decisively, many years ago, I determined that the Bible was to be the ultimate ground of appeal for me. This has not eliminated all the problems, but I have never been disappointed or disillusioned through the years. And over and over and over again, the validity of this decision has been confirmed as the Bible has proven itself to be absolutely reliable, without one single exception!

Whenever someone challenges the Bible, I always remember that I am faced with the choice of trading my faith in the Bible for faith in the man who is critical of it. And I have never met a man, or heard of a man, or read the works of a man whom I would rather trust than the Bible. Perhaps you think this naive. Very well, who or what do you trust for your final authority? You'll find the Bible to be absolutely trustworthy. Try it! "To whom shall we go? Thy Word is truth."

Jesus answered, "I am the way—and the

*truth and the life. No one comes to the
Father except through me."* —John 14:6

 Tuesday

Belief has to begin somewhere! Every man has
a starting point for his convictions. Even unbelief
begins with belief in something! Belief that the
Bible is untrustworthy, that Jesus Christ was just
a good man at best or may have been a myth,
that faith in God is irrelevant if not actually
destructive. (One university professor seriously
taught that belief in God sabotaged progress.)

Atheism, for example, believes in no God. Where
does atheism get that faith? Upon what authority
does atheism rely to support such belief?

The Christian begins with Jesus Christ—what
He said and did. He believes in the historicity of
Jesus, hence the Bible, the only adequate record
of Jesus' life and word and works. He believes the
Bible is trustworthy in its history.

Upon what does your belief (unbelief) rest?
Who do you believe rather than Jesus Christ? On
what book do you base your conviction if not the
Bible? Or do your convictions arise from within
yourself; do you begin with yourself, your own
mind, your own thoughts? In other words, are
you your own authority? If so, is what any other

man believes as right as you? Frankly, I do not know any person in history I would rather trust than Jesus Christ, any book I would rather rest my faith on than the Bible. Certainly I can have no confidence in any book which contradicts the Bible!

Lord, to whom shall we go? You have the words of eternal life. —John 6:68

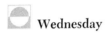 **Wednesday**

"I hope more Christians will take the broad view." by which he meant that all religious views are equally valid. And by inference, though he did not say it, that Jesus Christ is not unique. According to this view all men (except atheists) believe in God, even if they reject Jesus Christ as unique.

But what if God entered history in the person of Jesus Christ and chose to reveal Himself to the world that way? Or, to put it another way, what if Jesus Christ is the one incarnate revelation of the only God there is? How would you reconcile belief in God with rejection of Jesus Christ? In his self-awareness, Jesus understood Himself to be such a revelation of God: "Anyone who has seen me has seen the Father" (John 14:

9). The brilliant Jewish apostle, Paul, taught that God and Jesus were uniquely one. He wrote, "In Christ all the fullness of the Deity lives in bodily form" (Col. 2:9). In this he was in complete agreement with the other apostles.

When they accused Jesus of blasphemy for making Himself equal with God, He never denied it. Not even in His final trial which ended in His conviction and crucifixion. He accepted worship. The apostles rejected worship. If Jesus did not merit worship, He was infinitely less honorable than His apostles who refused to allow themselves to be worshiped. If Jesus is the final, fullest revelation of God, then Jesus is the broadest way to God, and only in that sense can the Christian take the broad view.

> *Jesus answered, "I am the way—and the truth and the life. No one comes to the Father except through me."* —John 14:6

 Thursday

Imagine John the Baptist doubting Jesus. Whoever would expect this man of all men to entertain any doubt whatsoever concerning Jesus Christ? Forerunner of the Messiah, his very birth a miracle anticipating the birth of the Savior. An unimpeachable background: his father a priest, his mother descended from Aaron, Israel's first high priest. They were righteous parents, records Dr. Luke, walking before the Lord in humility, keeping all the commandments, concerning the law blameless. What a legacy of gracious, authentic piety John must have had. His birth was announced by angels who predicted that many would rejoice at his greatness before the Lord, he would drink no wine or strong drink and would be filled with the Holy Spirit from his mother's womb. He was to turn many of the sons of Israel to the Lord their God and to make ready for the Lord a people prepared.

Remember the remarkable meeting between Elizabeth and Mary: Elizabeth carrying John in her womb, Mary carrying Jesus in hers; the sealing of the father's tongue until the child was named John. You can be sure John knew all these thrilling facts; they had been rehearsed over and over in his ears during boyhood and youth. He knew them by heart. He knew he was a miracle, commissioned by God to prepare the way for the Messiah. Recall his humility, how he scrupulously denied being the Messiah, insisted he was not worthy to stoop down and untie His shoestrings. Picture his painful embarrassment when Jesus came to him for baptism. Hear John cry, "Behold the Lamb of God that taketh away the sin of the world!" Yet this man doubted Jesus. If he could, anybody might!

Circumstances triggered the doubt: discouraged in prison, John began to wonder if all his glorious memories were really true. He needed reassurance. Faith is like this. It sometimes doubts, sometimes wonders, sometimes questions memory (circumstances do this to faith). Faith is exercised by doubts. Doubt is not sin! John doubted. Thomas doubted. And because of their doubts we have some of the most wonderful confirmations for faith. Jesus reassured John with a flurry of magnificent deeds (Luke 7:18-23). He met Thomas's doubt with a foolproof demonstration (John 20:24-28).

If any man will ... he shall know.
—John 7:17 (kjv)

 Friday

There are many kinds of idols in secularism—fame, wealth, popularity, prestige, power, influence—which take the place of God in a man's life! But there are other idols, far more dangerous in a sense, because they are so insidious, so subtle. There are idols in the lives of some men who would be classified as "conservative" or "fundamental" in their theology.

One thing that some good men make an idol of is creed! Creed becomes more important than Christ to some men. Creed takes the place of Christ Himself in their lives. They become creed-centered instead of Christ-centered. To be sure they would be the last to see this and the last to admit it, but that's just the point! That's why such idols are so dangerous. It is a master strategy of Satan: when he cannot keep a man from Christ, the next best thing is to get him more concerned over his belief about Christ than about Christ Himself.

There is a perfect type of this sort of idolatry in the New Testament. The Pharisee embodied it. He remained smug within the walls of his dogmatic position. Not even Jesus Christ could penetrate! The Pharisee had made a god out of works. He had made a god out of law. He had made a god out of tradition. He had made a god out of his own convictions. Not the truth, but his way of looking at it, became the absolute in his life. So much so that Jesus Christ had this to say to him: "You have made God's Word of no effect by teaching for doctrine the commandments of men." His traditions replaced God's Word!

Today there are otherwise strong Christian men who dogmatically equate truth with their expression of it. They've become bound by creed, by their little standards of conduct, by their opinions, by their convictions. They've crowned their creed as final and absolute, the last word. And in so doing, they have enthroned creed where only Christ has the right to rule.

Jesus Christ is bigger than any creed, than all creeds put together! Creed at best is man's way of defining and delineating the truth. Creed is a symbol for truth, but truth is always larger than its symbol. This is not to do away with creed. This is to give creed its proper place. Let's be sure we worship Christ Himself, not our limited understanding of Him!

Jesus answered, "I am . . . the truth."
—John 14:6

 Monday

"I feel no more responsibility for what people do with the weapons I sell them than an automobile manufacturer feels for traffic deaths." Thus bluntly rationalized one whose stock in trade is weapons of war. The ease with which he absolves himself from responsibility exposes a culpable blind spot in modern man's psychology. Where does responsibility lie?

Why, for example, should we make the "pusher" of narcotics responsible for the youth who are "hooked" by his product? Who's to blame for the

incalculable waste of man-hours, the human in-
dignities, smashed lives, broken homes, skid-row
derelicts, traffic deaths, and crime which are the
direct result of the liquor traffic? Certainly it is
not the men who manufacture and sell the liquor!
Who is responsible for the human destruction, the
blasted hopes, the hungry neglected kids, the
divorces, and suicides which are caused by the
gambling racket? Certainly not the professional
gambler, the casinos, the church bingo games!

How easily we get ourselves off the hook. With
what unmitigated hypocrisy we duck responsibility, invent scapegoats to take the onus off our
backs. War is inevitable; somebody will manufacture weapons; why shouldn't I take my share
of the profit? People are going to drink; somebody is going to make the stuff; I might as well
get in on the rake-off. People are going to take
drugs, gamble; what's wrong with grabbing a piece
of the "take"? Can you think of an easier way to
make a buck? (People murder, too, even when
there's a law against it. Why not legalize murder
and levy a murder tax. Think of the revenue!)
Sure there are loopholes in this argument: there's
a difference between heroin and whiskey, between war and gangland killing, between legal-
ized pari-mutuel and a bookie, between a posh
casino or church basement and a roving crap
game; but why should good people be accessories
after the fact? Why not refuse to traffic in human
degradation, no matter how much profit there is

born blind doesn't miss color. The man born deaf doesn't miss sound. The naked native in the jungle doesn't miss clothing. The man who has never been exposed to a concerto or symphony doesn't miss classical music. And generally speaking, the man who is not exposed to biblical preaching and teaching, to the life and ministry of Jesus, will be unaware of and often indifferent to the gift of eternal life which Christ gives.

I was awakened to my need for Christ out of sheer loneliness when I was twenty years old. Up to that time I was utterly oblivious to any need for Christ. The awareness came when I heard the Gospel preached. "Thou hast made us for thyself and restless are our hearts until they repose in thee," wrote St. Augustine, after he had come to Christ out of a profligate life in which he had been quite contented for years.

> *It is not the healthy who need a doctor, but the sick.* —Matthew 9:12

 **Wednesday**

"You don't drink!" expostulated the genial stranger at the reception with shocked surprise, "Why?" I guess I sounded like I was some kind of an odd-ball when I requested tomato juice instead of a cocktail. He seemed amazed at my lack of good judgment. "I'll be happy to tell you why I don't drink," I replied, "if you will tell me why you do. Why do you drink?" He blubbered a bit, mouthed something about social nicety, turned on his heel and zigzagged over to some of his cronies who were "normal." He didn't have an intelligent reason for drinking, however he wanted me to defend non-drinking as though it were unintelligent.

Strange, isn't it, that the drinker gets the idea a guy is a kind of "square" who refuses to saturate his body and brain with poison! It rarely occurs to a drinker that he has no constructive reason for drinking, though he expects the non-drinker to explain his "eccentricity." (Some drink just to please other drinkers, a vicious spiral that leads nowhere but down; others drink to forget, but the problem's still there when a man sobers up, only he's less capable of handling it.) No drinker has ever given me an intelligent reason for drinking, but the case for the non-drinker is airtight! He may not be a social lion, but he remembers what he did and said when the party's over! No one argues that alcoholic drinks are beneficial; in fact, there is considerable evidence that they are injurious to health and rob the sick person of desperately needed reserves with which to fight illness. Drinking doesn't sharpen a man's thinking; it dulls his responses, lowers his moral restraint, reduces his resistance to disease, shortens the life span of many, not to mention the incalculable bill in accidents and crime, loss of life and property, divorce and domestic difficulty, delinquency, loss of man-hours and efficiency directly due to drink. It runs into billions annually!

The evidence is all on the side of the non-drinker, yet the fellow who drinks seems bound to put him on the defensive, treat him as though he were some kind of a social monstrosity. (Interesting transposition of values!) Perhaps this is the drinker's way of salving his conscience in the presence of one whose concern for personal dignity, health, and stewardship makes him abstain. After all, the man who must spend many dollars weekly on drinks which have no constructive purpose has to find some self-justification, especially when he has trouble making ends meet financially.

> *Wine is a mocker, strong drink a brawler;*
> *and whoever is led astray by it is not*
> *wise.* —Proverbs 20:1

 Thursday

Accurate diagnosis is fundamental to cure! However excellent the prescription, it is inadequate for healing if based upon incorrect analysis of the symptoms. Hence the monotonous, aggravating failure of man's best efforts to solve his problems. His diagnosis is faulty! Human nature being what it is, and human pride persisting as it does, man refuses to believe anything but the best about himself. Human-like he blames everything but himself for his trouble. It's the government or education or the law or the Republicans or the Democrats or Protestants or Jews or Catholics or preachers or management or labor or the president or Congress or Communism or society in general and so on, ad nauseum! And man goes on in his blundering, egotistical way, puttering with the symptoms while the disease rages unchecked. The pay-off is precisely what we feel in this decade: complete frustration!

"We have harnessed the atom, but we will never make war obsolete until we find a force that will bridle the passions of men and nations," declared General Carlos Romulo of the Philippines while he was president of the United Nations. That's the real problem—the passions of men.

"Nothing outside a man can make him 'unclean' by going into him. Rather, it is what comes out of a man that makes him 'unclean.' . . . For from within, out of men's hearts, come evil thoughts, sexual immorality, theft, murder, adultery, greed, malice, deceit, lewdness, envy, slander, arrogance and folly. All these evils come from inside and make a man 'unclean'" (Mark 7:15, 21-23). The wisest Teacher who ever lived, who knew human nature as no other man, the Great Physician Himself, diagnosed the trouble as a malignancy within the human heart which infects everything man touches! "Man is his own biggest problem!" For this reason Jesus Christ came to this world to offer Himself as the cure for the disease of sin. He did not come just to teach; He came to redeem!

> *If anyone is in Christ, he is a new creation.* —2 Corinthians 5:17
> *I am not ashamed of the gospel, because it is the power of God for the salvation of everyone who believes.* —Romans 1:16

 Friday

Security and slavery are identical when security is one's goal! A man may be comfortable in his security, but he's not free. Not free even to have friends. If his security is in wealth, he can never really have friends because he never knows when he is accepted as a person, accepted for what he is, rather than what he has. He becomes increasingly fearful of being used. So he deepens and strengthens his defenses against people.

If security is in possessions, then attrition or loss represent disaster. And the irony is that one can never have enough wealth or enough possessions to be unthreatened. Every effort to protect such security builds some new, invisible wall around the life. That's slavery!

Emancipation comes when one lets go and relaxes his grip on things. Often the man who has little seeks his security in things: his total preoccupation is getting more, which can be even more enslaving than having much. Jesus enjoyed ultimate security, ultimate freedom, because His security was God!

> *Do not store up for yourselves treasures on earth, where moth and rust destroy, and where thieves break in and steal. But store up for yourselves treasures in heaven, where moth and rust do not destroy and where thieves do not break in and steal. For where your treasure is, there your heart will be also.*
> —Matthew 6:19-21

 Monday

How come "eternal vigilance is the price of freedom?" We accept this dogma without question, but have you ever thought it through? What kind of a world is it that requires such a deliberate, everlasting battle to preserve a state of affairs that everyone considers desirable? Why isn't freedom automatic? Why must we fight to win it, then keep battling to retain it? What's wrong anyway?

For that matter, why is it that the good never seems to come automatically? Whether it's raising children or running a business or gardening or sports or music or governing a nation or maintaining one's health, eternal vigilance is required. Let a child grow up "like Topsy," without discipline and instruction and nine times out of ten he'll go bad. Let a business run itself and it will go broke. Neglect a garden and weeds overrun it. Failure to train defeats the athlete. The musician who stops practicing gets rusty. Ignore elections and evil forces take over government. Let yourself go, neglect exercise, good food, proper rest, and the body suffers. But why? We take this principle for granted, yet at the same time many of us live a life that denies it.

On the basis of the evolutionary theory one would expect things to be getting better and better. The world should be becoming increasingly peaceful, etc. Evolution doesn't make sense when apart from serious, dogged effort on man's part; everything goes to pot, including man himself! Like a watch that runs down if it isn't kept wound, life disintegrates and falls apart if man doesn't strive continually and constantly to hold it together. Start taking things for granted and decay sets in; destruction is inevitable.

The Bible offers the correct diagnosis and the only adequate cure! The root of this incessant, inexorable destructive process is sin; the only adequate cure for sin is the sacrifice of the Son of God! For this reason man finds no solution to his problems as long as he insists on ignoring Jesus Christ. He alone is the cure for all man's ills: personal, domestic, social, industrial, racial, national, and international.

> *For God did not send his Son into the world to condemn the world, but to save the world through him.* —John 3:17

 Tuesday

Having spent three weeks in Europe, besieged with the criticism of U.S. "imperialism" in Asia, I want to record a few simple facts of history. At the end of World War II the great cities of Europe and Japan were in ruins, their lands ravaged. Their factories were rubble, their people exhausted. The U.S.A. had been spared war on her soil, her cities were thriving, her factories were geared to maximum production, her people were eager—their morale never higher. She had the most powerful army, navy, and air force in history, deployed throughout the world. And she alone had the atomic bomb!

The U.S.A. was in a position to occupy the

world—an unprecedented opportunity for total imperialism. What would Russia have done in that position? Germany? Japan? The question of course is hypothetical, but what the U.S.A. did is not! She retooled for peace. She joined hands with men everywhere to rebuild the world, not parsimoniously, but magnanimously, spontaneously, humbly. She poured her industrial, agricultural, and financial wealth into Europe, Asia, Latin America, and Africa—billions and billions and billions of dollars in aid. Undoubtedly her unprecedented prosperity today is due in part to this selfless sharing as a nation.

> "Our father's God, to thee,
>   Author of liberty,
>   To thee we sing;
>   Long may our land be bright
>   With freedom's holy light;
>   Protect us by thy might,
>   Great God, our King!"

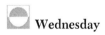 **Wednesday**

Communism cannot destroy America! Secularism may! Because secularism eats out the spiritual vitality of a nation, leaving inner debilitation, exhaustion, and emptiness. A spiritual America is a strong America, invulnerable to Communism. Communism cannot compete with a spiritually strong society. She must first find ways of canceling out or neutralizing spiritual stamina. Communism knows how to capitalize on spiritual weakness.

Secularism softens a society, making it a pushover for outside forces. Consider this advertisement by *Warner & Swasey* of Cleveland (*Newsweek*, March 31, 1958): "It wasn't the Goths that defeated Rome. It was the free circuses! Luxuries, power, indulgence had made the once-tough Roman people soft. To stay popular, their emperors gave them more and more of the ease they craved, free bread, free circuses, easier living. So the Romans softened up themselves for the ambitious, hard-working barbarians. And in 410 AD the greatest nation the world had ever seen was invaded and destroyed. The greedy cry of 'something for nothing,' the stupid whine of 'somebody else should sacrifice, not me' could do exactly the same for this nation!"

American leaders admit the need for spiritual vitality, while at the same time they are inclined to justify the neglect of spiritual practices on the grounds that they are too busy. Their preoccupation with business may be the cause of their loss of the very enterprise that demands their attention. As long as men excuse themselves from their spiritual responsibilities because they are too busy with material matters, they are setting the stage for their own defeat by material forces. Men who are too busy for God and the church and the Bible and prayer are too busy! Daily such men are driving America nearer to the point where Communism can push through the crust of spiritual culture that has become sterile and static.

If my people who are called by my name humble themselves, and pray and seek my face, and turn from their wicked ways, then I will hear from heaven, and will forgive their sin and heal their land.
—2 Chronicles 7:14

 Thursday

Japanese gardeners have a way of producing miniature plants. They grow to maturity, greatly reduced in size. They are dwarfed, subnormal! The gardeners do this simply by severing the taproot, leaving the plant to survive on auxiliary roots.

In which there is a parable on America. Giant that the U.S.A. is among the world of nations, she is still young, still in her adolescence. And while yet in her childhood she is fighting for survival. Before reaching her maturity she faces premature death, extinction! Because she has severed her taproot! She is relying on subordinate, auxiliary roots to supply her with nourishment and strength. And they are not sufficient!

This is undebatable: America owes its birth to a living, vital, dynamic faith in Jesus Christ, Savior and Lord. The documents of her founding are filled with this faith! This is the taproot of true Americanism! Today men talk about freedom and work for it, while at the same time they utterly ignore Jesus Christ and His claim on them. They wonder why freedom eludes their finest efforts. It is not strange! For freedom, the American brand, comes from Jesus Christ and His Gospel. It's a matter of record, confirmed again and again in history, that the American way of life with all its implications is a direct product of Christian faith. Our economic, financial, and political structures are all dependent on Christian faith. Torn from this taproot, rigor mortis sets in. Collapse and extinction are inevitable!

If only men would think. If they would quit shadowboxing, quit beating the air with their schemes, their slogans, their crusades which bypass Jesus Christ. They fight a losing battle unless they return to that which made America possible in the first place! There's a direct correlation between sound economics, sound finance, sound politics, and Christian faith! Rejection of Christ and His Way is the mother of false economics, false finance, government without consent of the governed. We might as well face it.

As long as men in positions of leadership refuse to acknowledge this, refuse to humble themselves before God, refuse to confess their sin, and refuse to turn to Christ in repentance, no matter what else they do, we're doomed! That's that! This is the personal obligation of every thinking American.

> *If my people who are called by my name humble themselves, and pray and seek my face, and turn from their wicked ways, then I will hear from heaven, and will forgive their sin and heal their land.*
> —2 Chronicles 7:14

 Friday

Give the "radical" a break! Remove the establishment which provokes him, the system which frustrates him. Let him start from scratch. Let him begin with the fundamentals, with the raw earth: no pollution, no bureaucracy, no police, no army, no politicians, no middle class, no older generation, no tradition, no history, no past! Nothing to interfere with his plans, just good old mother earth in her pristine glory.

Then let him make his demands, demonstrate, revolt. He'll discover that nothing in life is payable on demand. In its simplest form life is costly, requiring work as the fundamental necessity.

Blood, sweat, and tears are built into creation—the unrelenting prerequisite to existence. Life is an investment, with returns dependent upon input. If he thinks about this, he might appreciate the luxury of a "system" which supports him while he violates it. He might be able to see beyond his revolution to the nothingness which will haunt him if he is successful with his destruction. He may understand that peaceful change, however slow and painful, is the rational, fruitful way.

> *And God said, "Be fruitful and multiply, and fill the earth and subdue it; and have dominion over the fish of the sea and over the birds of the air and over every living thing."* —Genesis 1:28

 Monday

"If history teaches that, then history is wrong!" A Presbyterian minister said that to me when we were discussing the relative merits of social action and the Gospel of Jesus Christ. I had quoted from the eminent Bible expositor, G. Campbell Morgan, who wrote that history confirmed the fact that the church had had its greatest social impact on the world when it had been most faithful to the Gospel of Christ and preached the salvation of individual man. The minister's rebuttal was the incredible statement with which this letter opens. Not much chance of "dialogue" with that kind of logic, but it illustrates what is being done in history today. Whether it is the facts concerning our Lord Jesus Christ as reported in the thoroughly reliable historical records of the New Testament or history in general, one of the contradictory tendencies of contemporary man is his break with the past.

Recall the desecration and destruction of the birthplace of Confucius by the Red Guard of mainland China. It is inconceivable that two thousand years of proud civilization could be so wastefully, so ingloriously repudiated, just because it did not conform to the views of Red China's failing leader. But that's the spirit of our adolescent age. If history doesn't agree with us, then so much the worse for history. This is not progress; this is consummate retrogression.

Much of the revolutionary spirit of the present has lost sight of purposeful goals. It is vindictive, destructive, and self-defeating. Revolution that becomes a vendetta with the past is devolution! Revolution that demands change while it repudiates continuity may "get even" with the past, but it holds no promise for the future. This is not to defend the status quo; no thoughtful person does today. But it is to say that we owe much to history, and our most hopeful future lies in learning from it and moving ahead with the lessons.

> *Do not think that I have come to abolish*
> *the Law or the Prophets; I have not come*
> *to abolish them, but to fulfill them.*
> —Matthew 5:17

 Tuesday

National pride is not the need of the hour. National humiliation is! This is not to ignore all that is good about the United States. Indeed it is to recognize the good—and its Source! It is to remember what we so easily forget, the unusual blessing of God upon us from our exceptional beginnings. It is to give credit where credit is due.

We have presumed upon the goodness of God and behaved as if we ourselves are responsible for our greatness, as if we are a specially qualified race, superior, invincible. We have allowed military victories, increasing wealth, unprecedented technological progress, and industrial advancement to blind us to the religious roots of our birth. National pride is our greatest danger now! National repentance is essential!

"It is the duty of nations of men to own their dependence upon the overruling power of God,

ways of escaping the problem—sweeping the dirt under the rug. It is, in fact, abdication! We get the matter off our hands into the committee's; then it's someone else's responsibility. As the power decreases, we increase the outlets until there's not enough energy left to push the power to the outlet. That is the way a movement becomes machinery and the machinery grinds to a halt. The next step is a monument! Period!

Why don't we face ourselves honestly, admit we are without spiritual power, and acknowledge our impotency, instead of multiplying organizations, committees, crusades; in place of resolutions and revolt, demands and demonstrations, let us repent of our sin, our selfishness, our pride, our preoccupation with things temporal, our neglect of things eternal. Let us listen to Christ and come out from behind our pious, ecclesiastical facade. Let us recognize our inadequacy without Him, our invincibility in Him. Let's quit being satisfied with man's best and not rest until we see and hear and feel God at work. Let's recognize that nothing that is possible can save us. Only the impossible is adequate!

Humanity languishes for a demonstration of the mighty acts of God in our generation. We who are God's servants have been busying ourselves far too long with the petty products of our own little hands, our ingenuity and management. We need to confess our failure, receive His forgiveness, wash ourselves clean in the "blood of the

Lamb," and become the human instruments of the divine power which alone can accomplish God's eternal purposes in history.

> *Not by might, nor by power, but by my Spirit, says the Lord of hosts.*
> —Zechariah 4:6

 Thursday

Man is one! There's nothing plainer than that in Scripture. Take the Bible seriously and you believe in the unity of man. Man is one in creation. All men have a common ancestry, descend from the same parents. As the Apostle Paul put it, "From one man he made every nation of men, that they should inhabit the whole earth" (Acts 17:26).

Man is one in sin. "Just as sin entered the world through one man, and death through sin, and in this way death came to all men, because all sinned" (Rom. 5:12). Man is one in creation, one in sin! But paradoxically, sin is what divides man. Sin alienates—alienates man from God and man. The deepest division in humanity is not race or language or color; the deepest division is sin. If it were not for his sin, man would not be divided by race or language or color.

God anticipated this division before he created man, planned the remedy, and provided it in the person of Jesus Christ. The cure for sin is the grace of God in Christ. Which is precisely what the Apostle Paul makes clear in Romans 5:12-21; the only thing more powerful than sin is the grace of God. Grace, when accepted by man, changes him and makes him one with all others who have accepted grace, unites them in one family, one body. Men who remain divided betray the fact that the grace of God does not reign in their lives. Jesus said,

> *All men will know that you are my disciples if you love one another.*
>
> —John 13:35

 Friday

"Foolish consistency is the hobgoblin of little minds." Religious consistency can be diabolical! Devotion to God and consistency to religious convictions are not identical. Consistency to religious convictions may produce a fanatic; devotion to God will produce a saint!

The Son of God was the most inconsistent Man who ever lived by the standards of the Pharisees. He was continually breaking their rules, continually in hot water with the religionists of His day.

Because they were doggedly consistent to their convictions. He was utterly devoted to God's will. Their convictions had become a fetish. They no longer held their convictions; their convictions held them! Their godliness was hollow: it possessed the form, but was without power. The fresh, honest, God-devoted life of Jesus was utterly enigmatic to them. By their standards, Jesus was not only a blasphemer—He was dangerous! Their religious convictions had become their god. They were idol worshipers as much as the Greek pagans who had altars to every conceivable deity, even an altar to "the unknown god." Their idol was their dogma! God had been expelled from their religion. They gave Him lip service, but their hearts were far from Him.

In fact, their religion had become the enemy of God. Their convictions made them hostile to God's way. Whatever their excuse, their religion was the reason they crucified Jesus. And religious conviction has been crucifying Christ in every generation since. Religious conviction is continually nailing righteousness to a cross! This does not mean that authentic devotion is without dogmatic substance, but it does mean that one never equates his doctrinal position with almighty God. Doctrine, essential as it is, remains subordinate to the Person of Christ.

Why do you call me "Lord, Lord," and do not do what I say?   —Luke 6:46

An amusing anecdote illustrates the approach some men make to truth. It concerns a group of sophisticated skeptics who were enjoying a discussion on religion at the expense of a faithful Christian who was trying vainly to defend his position. From the standpoint of the skeptics, the Christian was simple and naive and held a faith that bordered on superstition. From their exalted intellectual position they were trying to straighten him out, wise him up. Among them was a doctor who finally applied the *coup de grace* with a battery of questions: "Have you ever seen religion? Have you ever tasted it? Heard it? Smelled it?" To each the Christian replied, "No!" "Then have you ever felt religion?" "Yes" replied the Christian. "I say this man is a fraud" said the doctor, "for he accepts as true that which he has experienced with only one of his five senses." Said the Christian to the doctor, "Have you ever seen, tasted, heard, smelled pain?" "No!" was the doctor's reply. "Well have you felt pain?" asked the Christian. "To be sure" answered the M.D. Then suggested the Christian, "You have been guilty of fraudulent practice, for you have been taking money for years for relieving something which you have experienced with only one of your five senses!"

It would be ridiculous were it not so utterly

pathetic, the number of self-styled intellectuals who repudiate the greatest thing in the world on just as unstable a basis as the skeptic in the story. No one has ever seen an atom, yet we believe it exists. No one has ever seen electricity, yet we use it daily. We believe because we see the effects. And there is manifold evidence for belief in God. The whole weight of evidence upholds this belief. So much in fact that the Bible declares, "The fool says . . ., 'There is no God'" (Ps. 14:1). Fools disregard evidence either because they lack the ability to reason, or they do it deliberately. The evidence for Jesus Christ and His Gospel is strong, weighty, and convincing! Only the man who refuses to consider the evidence remains untouched. As a matter of fact, this is at the root of unbelief. Not that men cannot believe, but that they will not! They simply refuse. And then justify their skepticism or secularism or indifference by ludicrous arguments.

If any man's will is to do his (God's) will,
he shall know. —John 7:17 (RSV)

 Tuesday

Hell has no exit! There's no way out for the man who elects it as his final destiny. Hard as this may be to accept, and incompatible as it may seem to an "enlightened Christendom," for one whose authority is the Bible, the fact remains—hell has no exit.

Some other biblical facts, however, ought to be considered as well. Hell was intended for the devil and his angels (Matt. 25:41). God neither delights in nor desires any man in hell. "It is not his will that any should perish." But God created man as a free moral agent, not a puppet, and it is part of man's freedom to choose to conform to God's will or to reject it. That man who desires not the will of God now would find it intolerable in eternity.

Like heaven, hell is each man's option. God has, in fact, done all in His power to keep man from hell. That was the purpose of Christ's entrance into history. That is why this perfect One submitted to the ignominy of a trial by His creatures and death by crucifixion like a common criminal. He was "the lamb of God that taketh away the sin of the world."

Which recalls an experience of a clergyman friend. He was seated in a train reading his Bible when a man entered, noticed the Bible, and passed down the aisle looking for a seat. None being available, he reluctantly returned to the vacant one next to the preacher with his Bible. My friend remained silent as he read, which seemed unbearable to the man. Finally he blurted out, "Suppose you're a preacher?" My friend confirmed his fears. "Suppose you believe God's going to send everybody to hell?" To which my friend replied, "No, God sends no man to hell." Considerably relieved, the man relaxed, at which time my preacher friend reminded him, "There's a cross over the door of hell, and God's Son hung on that cross. It was meant to keep men out of hell. You can only get into hell by ignoring that cross." God did His best. The choice is each man's!

> *For God did not send his Son into the world to condemn the world, but to save the world through him. Whoever believes in him is not condemned, but whoever does not believe stands condemned already because he has not believed in the name of God's one and only Son.*
> —John 3:17-18

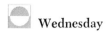 **Wednesday**

Either God is or He isn't. If He isn't, there's no use pretending He is. The atheist can stop his war against God; it certainly doesn't make sense to fight against something that is nonexistent. We can stop being disappointed in man. He's just an animal; his law is that of the jungle; one does not expect moral behavior from him. Morality is an illusion. Why be bothered about it? The grave is the end. Get all you can, however you can, whenever you can, while the getting is good!

Forget the future; live for now! For that matter, forget the past. If God is not, we are the product of an impersonal, evolutionary process and we have nothing to learn from history. Hope is a myth; take what life offers. Make the most of right now!

But if God is, then let's behave like He is! Let's practice what we say we believe. Let's seek to know God's will and do it. Let's live with eternity in view. Let's endure as "seeing the invisible." Let's "seek first his kingdom and his righteousness." And let the chips fall where they may!

> *For although they knew God, they neither glorified him as God nor gave thanks to him, but their thinking became futile and their foolish hearts were darkened. Although they claimed to be wise, they became fools.* —Romans 1:21-22

 Thursday

Don't allow your experience with Jesus Christ to be limited by your understanding of Him!

Really knowing Jesus goes far beyond the bounds of theological knowledge. As a matter of fact, there are probably theologians whose great minds have mastered the doctrines of the various Christian traditions who are quite unfamiliar with Jesus personally. They know a lot about Jesus, but they do not know Him! An illiterate may know Jesus in a way the scholar never can, if the scholar insists on limiting his knowledge to intellectual apprehension.

The plain fact is that the disciples of Jesus knew Him well long before they could understand Him. They accepted Him, followed Him, loved Him, and served Him without ever being able to explain Him. In many ways He was an enigma to them, but they never allowed their perplexity to stand in the way of a personal relationship. They enjoyed a thrilling fellowship with Him amidst the mystery of His words and works. Their theology about Him, whatever it may have been, came long after they had felt the impact of His life and love.

What a pity that there are so many today who call themselves Christian yet who refuse to take one step with Jesus beyond the point where reason leads. In so doing, whether they realize it or not, they are enthroning reason over against Jesus Christ, allowing their minds to be the judge of Jesus. They are not accepting Him at face value; they are accepting only their limited understanding of Him. They do not worship Him;

they worship only their views of Him! And they deprive themselves of the indescribable benefits which accrue to the man who walks with Jesus in confidence and trust. Authentic faith is never achieved at the sacrifice of intellect; but the intellect too often sacrifices a delightful personal relationship with Jesus which comes through faith.

> *Then Jesus declared, "I am the bread of life. He who comes to me will never go hungry, and he who believes in me will never be thirsty."* —John 6:35

 Friday

God has not abdicated!

The agony of our late twentieth century is evidence of the accuracy of the Bible's statements concerning the last days and an encouragement to look for the return of Jesus Christ! The space race, the mad rush to stockpile atomic weapons, the frustration and futility of diplomacy, the unpredictable eruption of trouble spots like pus sacs, the increase of industrial tension, the acceleration of crime and festering social malignancy, the hot breath of nationalism and revolution, the sickening, unrelenting, inexorable threat of thermonuclear war, these are not the death rattle of

Christian civilization; they are the birth pangs of Christian fulfillment!

Universal trouble does not spell doom. It proclaims victory! "The whole creation is on tiptoe to see the wonderful sight of the sons of God coming into their own. The world of creation cannot as yet see reality . . . yet it has been given hope. And the hope is that in the end the whole of created life will be rescued from the tyranny of change and decay, and have its share in that magnificent liberty which can only belong to the children of God! It is plain to anyone with eyes to see that at the present time all created life groans in a sort of universal travail . . . while we wait for that redemption of our bodies which will mean that at last we have realized our full sonship in Christ" (Rom. 8:19-23, Phillips).

Scoffers mock at the thought of Christ's return on the grounds that the church has waited for this event for nineteen centuries, and this very scoffing fulfills Bible prediction. It is one of the signs (2 Pet. 3:3-5). Nothing is more certain than Christ's triumphal re-entry into history, and it is 1900 years nearer than when it was first promised! Today the whole universe languishes for the return of the Prince of Peace.

The kingdom of the world has become the kingdom of our Lord and of his Christ. —Revelation 11:15
Jesus Christ is Lord!

"The unconsecrated wealth of Christians is the greatest hindrance to the church's progress!"*

In thirteen words that astounding statement describes the insidious nature of materialism, the most destructive force in history.

Despite all our Lord had to say about the "deceitfulness of riches," about the difficulty of "rich men entering the kingdom of heaven," that one "cannot serve God and money"; despite the cosmic tragedy of hunger and poverty in much of the world today; despite the clear judgment of God upon His people when they ignore the cries of the oppressed, neglect the poor, the widow, and the orphan; and despite the biblical truth that God owns everything and loans it to man to hold and use for His glory and the benefit of his fellowman, there are multitudes of Christians who not only have far more than they can ever need, but who with a passion pursue acquisition as though their lives depended upon it. Needs are met, but luxuries are demanded; then the luxuries become needs and more luxuries are sought. Instead of being channels of divine blessing to the world, they become reservoirs dammed up and holding back the blessing. Satiated but unsatisfied by consumer obsession, they continue to seek more.

*Tithing Digest, published by Layman Tithing Foundation, Chicago, Illinois.

And never is there enough! May God send an awakening that will crumble the dams of selfishness and greed.

> *No one can serve two masters. Either he will hate the one and love the other, or he will be devoted to the one and despise the other. You cannot serve God and Money.* —Matthew 6:24

 Tuesday

A certain pastor, on the occasion of the annual stewardship campaign, wrote a letter to the members of his church, upon receipt of which one man replied immediately and with considerable rancor, "According to your concept, Christianity is just one continual give, give, give." Disturbed by this reaction, the pastor sat down to write a devastating reply. But as he thought and prayed about it, he found himself thinking, *that man is dead right! Christianity is one continual give!*

Instead of a scorching letter and rebuke, the pastor wrote the following: "Dear Friend: Thank you for the finest definition of Christianity that I have ever seen. Christianity is one continual give, give, give. That is the way it all began. God

207

gave. He gave His only Son. The Son gave. He gave His life upon the cross for our sins. His disciples gave. They left their homes and businesses to devote full time to telling the good news. Most of the twelve died a martyr's death. Down the centuries, the work of Christ has prospered in proportion to the extent that Christians have learned to give, give, give."

There is no way to improve upon that pastor's letter. Jesus said, "It is more blessed to give than to receive." The blessing is all on the side of the giver; the parched, blanched, scorched, barren life accrues to the one who has not learned to give. There is no terminus to the life of the man who for Christ's sake decides to give himself away, and keep on giving. "Give until it hurts," someone has said. No! Giving that hurts is trivial. The man that is pained by giving is the man who gives as little as possible. "Give until it feels good" is far wiser counsel.

You can't outgive God! Christianity is give, give, give, and the Christian who has discovered this enjoys a life abundantly rich and fruitful. In the words of the proverb, "One man gives freely, yet grows all the richer; another withholds what he should give, and only suffers want" (Prov. 11:24). Jesus said,

> *Give, and it will be given to you. A good measure, pressed down, shaken together and running over, will be poured into*

your lap. For with the measure you use,
it will be measured to you.   —Luke 6:38

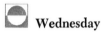 **Wednesday**

"I don't believe in making pledges to the church," the man said as the pledge cards were passed. "It isn't right to be committed ahead of time in giving." Sounds reasonable, even a bit pious at first. Until you begin to think it through. This same man is paying for his house on time. He is committed years ahead on the payments. He got his furniture this way also, and the appliances, and his car. In fact, he can't remember when he wasn't making time payments. He doesn't mind being committed ahead of time when it comes to his own comforts; he's got his salary spent before he receives it every month. But when it comes to the church, when it comes to the things which pertain to God, he practices an amazingly cautious economic attitude.

The excuses men give for not pledging to Christian causes would be humorous if they were not so terribly tragic. What an index to the unimportance some men attach to the kingdom of God. Houses, furniture, appliances, cars, etc., come first. After that, if there's any left over, God may come in for a small share. We don't really take Jesus

Christ seriously when He admonishes, "Seek you first his kingdom and his righteousness." We call Him "Lord," but we don't live as though He is! We sound pious, but we manage our money like pagans. We believe in thrift, especially when it comes to the church or missions. But how careful are we about our pleasures and possessions?

> *No one can serve two masters. Either he will hate the one and love the other, or he will be devoted to the one and despise the other. You cannot serve both God and Money.* —Matthew 6:24

 Thursday

You can't do everything for everybody—but you can do something for someone! The massive nature of our social problems needs not paralyze the concerned man. He cannot solve the problem of crime, but he can visit one prisoner, be a brother or father to him, give him the love and care for lack of which he may be behind bars.

He cannot solve the problem of poverty, but he can help one poor man or family, give them the assistance they need—not just money, but counsel, and encouragement. He cannot solve the problem of pollution, but he can stop littering and pick up trash when he sees it. He cannot stop the drug traffic, but he can help one lonely youth, hooked and filled with despair. And he can get behind others who are giving themselves to serving those in need; he can support them with his money and prayers. He cannot stop war, but he can be a man of peace in his home, his office, among his friends and peers.

He can be an agent of reconciliation and love wherever he is! Depending upon massive solutions leads to nowhere! Just as bad as the hippie is the adult who cops out and does nothing when he can do something! Jesus' answer is not the monolithic, institutional response, but the aggregate of individual disciples moving in His love to serve people in need. It doesn't take unusual prophetic insight to envision what a difference it would make in our world if each of us became a committee of one to do what he could where he is in obedience to Jesus Christ.

Whatever you did for one of the least of these brothers of mine, you did for me.
　　　　　　　　　　　　　—Matthew 25:40

 Friday

"Hurry is the word for today! We do not have

forever!" Such pressure may be deceptive, indicating a lack of balance between awareness of the need and confidence in God's adequacy. One can examine with meticulous care the New Testament record of Jesus' life without finding any evidence of hysteria on His part. And He knew He had but three years to fulfill His mission. His concern for the need of man is unequaled. His total conformity to the will of the Heavenly Father is indisputable. He knew the world of His time better than any contemporary; He was aware more than any other of the desperate need for divine intervention. Yet His life was characterized (in the words of one devotional writer) by "exquisite leisure."

Jesus never wasted time, but He never allowed Himself to be pressed into panic either. He knew the abysmal need for the light and life and love of God in the world better than any other man before or since His time; but He enjoyed complete confidence in the providential, over-arching care of Almighty God and the perfection of His plan in history. Jesus Christ was delicately sensitive to the human dilemma; He was likewise sublimely relaxed in the will of God. He bore man's burden, shared man's suffering as no other, but He trusted in the Father's timing.

Our day demands greater emulation of our Lord in this respect. This does not justify laziness or apathy (which are inexcusable for the Christian), but it does urge deeper confidence in God's faithful and unfailing love. Give us men who are realistically awake to the explosive issues and are alert to their obligation, but who nevertheless demonstrate unbending faith in the unalterable integrity of God. Such men will not be in a hurry! But they will deliver the goods to the right place, at the right time, in the right way! With feet on the ground, their hearts in touch with heaven, they'll be God's appointed men for God's appointed hour!

> *He who believes will not be in haste!*
> —Isaiah 28:16
> *Be not be anxious about anything.*
> —Philippians 4:6

 Monday

Two articles appearing in the *San Francisco Chronicle* on the same day give gruesome insight into the present state of Western culture. The first, by Alistair Cooke of the *Manchester Guardian,* was headed "Calcutta Slums, Squalid Sore of Poverty." He described the jolt received by a Westerner when the "heavy abstractions" of poverty, illiteracy, disease, heat, etc., suddenly become "flesh." "For your own sanity," he wrote, "you very soon learn to accept, and to pass by, the nightly bundles of rags, shored up against dark tree trunks in the country and the buildings in the cities, which occasionally stir and stretch and turn into prostrate human beings. A quarter of the people live in slum huts," said Cooke, "and almost 80 per cent of these house five families with a common privy and a water tap (where they are lucky enough to have either), and living room for each human of about seven feet by five."

He continued, "Every night the ambulances clatter around the rough streets, and when a body with thighs like bamboo poles refuses to be kicked into protest, it is turned over and found to be dead and hauled off to the mortuary. Two to three hundred a night of such corpses is the grudging figure. Not 20 yards from the platforms of the railway stations crowds of ragged families were camped on the stone flags. With one hand a young mother stirred a rusty pot of rice over a few smoking twigs and with the other she held an infant no bigger than an embryo to a breast as shrivelled as an old hot water bottle. Five other naked children, weighing anything from 10 to 50 pounds, fiddled and yawned around her." And so on, and on, and on.

The second article was entitled "An Author's 5-Day Bash, Party of the Century." It was the story of an American host and globetrotter who urged "his 200 overseas guests to take plenty of steam baths if they want to survive the five-day binge." Held in Copenhagen, the party celebrated its host's fiftieth birthday; he said he had been "saving up since 1951" for this party. Eighty guests arrived from America by chartered jet. Said the article, "The Danish capital has seen nothing so lavish or meticulously organized in many a day. Steam baths are available around the clock at the Copenhagen Health Center, described in the party brochure as 'a two-minute stagger from the hotel.'" The host and his wife had booked into a Danish sanitarium. "We plan to stay a week, recovering," he said. According to him, "This is a party without motive. The hell with selling books, the hell with publicity for me, the hell with everything but having fun." 'Nuff said!

> *Do not be deceived: God cannot be mocked. A man reaps what he sows. The one who sows to please his sinful nature, from that nature will reap destruction; the one who sows to please the Spirit, from the Spirit will reap eternal life.*
> —Galatians 6:7-8

 Tuesday

You don't have a problem or perplexity that the Son of God is not more than adequate to meet! Perhaps you don't think so right now, but wouldn't you be a fool to disregard Him if there is that possibility? Does indifference to Christ make sense when it involves the risk of depriving yourself of the resources He delights in lavishing upon you? Any intelligent man is interested in reserves for contingencies! It is consistent with good business practice to investigate reasonable ways and means whereby reserves for contingencies can be had.

In His Son, God offers you unlimited resources for any imaginable need you will have in the foreseeable future and beyond. If you are wise, you seek qualified specialists to give you counsel and direction in those areas where you need assistance. Why not seek the counsel and direction of the Supreme Specialist in life? Nothing is more certain than His availability! This is the central fact of the Christian faith! If you don't believe this, if this is a lot of foolishness to your mind, what is the basis of your disbelief?

Have you tried the Son of God and found Him inadequate? Have you called to Him and found He did not answer? Or are you merely uninformed, ignorant of the Scriptures, biased, stubborn, and proud? If you doubt the relevance of Jesus Christ, at least you owe it to yourself to investigate the possibility that He is right, that those who have tried Christ and found Him adequate have a point. You have nothing to gain (and everything to lose) by complacency or bullheadedness. Prove to your own satisfaction whether or not Jesus Christ is what He claimed and will do what He promised. This doesn't require a course in theology; it requires only an open mind, a willing heart, and a few minutes a day given to the New Testament and prayer.

> *And my God will meet all your needs according to his glorious riches in Christ Jesus.* —Philippians 4:19

 Wednesday

He was going to crack 300 miles an hour, then quit racing. He did. And he quit! But not the way he intended. At 310 miles an hour, Donald Campbell's jet hydroplane, *Bluebird,* disintegrated. A dramatic reminder that the most careful plans of men are fallible and had best be left in other hands.

Not that a man should not plan; but he ought to plan with God in mind; ought to commit the care and keeping of his soul to the Savior of men. This too is an intelligent part of foresight. Whatever else Donald Campbell's untimely death teaches us, it speaks of the uncertainty of life; the sobering fact that death may visit a man at any moment, when least expected, at the moment of triumph as well as defeat. Death is no respecter of persons, and it does not always announce its arrival. Human biography is filled with the records of the finest plans man can lay interrupted by death.

Then why not do all one can to prepare for such an eventuality? If there were no provision one could make, neglect would be excusable. But Jesus Christ entered history to guarantee a deathless hope to any man who would receive it. You've made provision for your family in the event of your death, but what have you done for the eternal welfare of your own soul? What strange irrational process causes you to ignore this?

> *Whoever puts his faith in the Son has eternal life, but whoever rejects the Son will not see that life, for God's wrath remains on him.* —John 3:36
> *To all who received him, to those who believed in his name, he gave the right to become children of God.* —John 1:12

 Thursday

Possessions bless life or curse it, depending on how one handles them. One of man's greatest difficulties is to distinguish between possessions and ownership. In the Bible, ownership is always

God's; He bears the right of eminent domain over the whole universe! He entrusts to man the use of things during his lifetime, and the way man handles this trusteeship leads to blessing or curse in his life. Man possesses—never owns! God owns and gives to man to possess. Possessions are held and used for the glory of God and the benefit of mankind.

Man enters the world at birth with nothing; he exits at death with nothing. In between entrance and exit, life is spent acquiring more or less. What man does with what he acquires is the key to fullness of life. When acquisition becomes a goal in life, possessions become destructive to the one who holds them. He crosses the invisible line where he no longer possesses but is possessed by his holdings. He becomes a slave to things, which is materialism at its insidious worst!

"Naked I came from my mother's womb, and naked shall I return thither; the Lord gave and the Lord has taken away; blessed be the name of the Lord" (Job 1:21) was Job's conviction. And Jesus said,

> *It is easier for a camel to go through the eye of a needle than for a rich man to enter the kingdom of God.*
> *No one can serve two masters. . . . You cannot serve God and Money.*
> —Matthew 20:24; 6:24

In the final analysis, men go to pieces because their god is not big enough! They are overwhelmed by circumstances, victimized by life, because their god is at the mercy of history. Every man has a god! Every man believes in something which takes precedence over everything else. It is that for which he strives most—his priority; all other issues are subordinate, made to serve the big goal. It has supreme value; all other values are secondary.

This god may be success, however the man interprets it, in terms of fame, fortune, personal power, etc. Some men worship pleasure and evaluate all their activities on the basis of their pleasure return. A man's god may be himself! With consummate conceit he boasts, "I am the master of my fate. I am the captain of my soul." Every issue is decided by the ego reference, "What's in it for me?" Self is at the center of all he thinks and says and does.

Man is only as strong as that which is first in his life! Jesus' humanity was based on total conformity to God's will. "I do only that which pleases him," He said. That's perfect humanity. Invincible humanity!

Seek first his kingdom and his righteousness. —Matthew 6:33

Money talks! It says a great deal about the man who handles it. It speaks of his value system and confirms or contradicts what he professes. It is an infallible index of his priorities. It tells where his focus is, where his major concerns lie, what he considers minor or trivial.

It says a great deal about his attitude toward his family. It speaks of his view of work, whether what he produces is important or whether he's just working to make a buck. It reveals his true religion—tells the world who his God really is! It indicates what he thinks about his church, where he puts his faith, what his goals in life are. It speaks of his concern or indifference to his community.

It tells what a man thinks of himself, whether he has eternal value or simply temporal value; whether he thinks of himself as a spiritual being or as a biological creature—just an animal.

Money talks. And there is very little about a man which it does not reveal. There is no more accurate or penetrating index to a man's character.

No one can serve two masters. Either he will hate the one and love the other, or he will be devoted to the one and despise the other. You cannot serve both God and Money. —Matthew 6.24

What is the highest motive for the Christian? Is it to be godly? Self-willed determination to be godly may be the worst enemy of Jesus Christ. This incentive, in fact, led to the first sin ever committed by a human being. Eve, convinced that she would be like God if she ate the forbidden fruit, capitulated to satanic enticement. In her determination to be like God, she disobeyed Him and served the devil! This motivation led Saul of Tarsus to be the arch-persecutor of the church. In his passion for godliness he did his utmost to liquidate all Christians.

Is righteousness the highest motive? This was the essence of Pharisaism: preoccuption with their own virtues mobilized the Pharisees against Jesus Christ until finally, in their frustration and hostility, they engineered His crucifixion. Is the supreme goal to be a soul winner? This ambition will lead one of two ways: either to commercialism and the pride of "success" based upon external results, or to frustration and despair over one's failure to see the results someone else is getting. Emphasis on "fruit" when it is equated with souls "won" is always perilous, for it tends to lead away from abiding in Christ. One may see "fruit" in this sense without abiding, but he cannot fail to be fruitful when he abides. To abide in Christ is to be fruitful. Jesus said so!

There is only one legitimate primary motive for the Christian. That is to be Christ's! Just to be His! Oneness with Christ is the only safe and fulfilling motive. Be His and godliness, righteousness, and fruitfulness are inevitable.

> *I am the vine; you are the branches. If a man remains in me and I in him, he will bear much fruit; apart from me you can do nothing.* —John 15:5

 Wednesday

Things are not good or bad in and of themselves; it is the touch of man that makes the difference. In our human pride we refuse to acknowledge this and blame inanimate things for our dilemma.

Nuclear energy is neither moral nor immoral. It's how man uses it. It's "mod" today to blame the system, whatever is meant by that. But systems are neutral and become evil or good depending upon how men use them. Of course some systems are better than others. Dictatorship is the most efficient political system, but where do you find a benevolent dictator?

Democracy is slow and inefficient, but it guarantees the greatest freedom and opportunity for the greatest number. You don't get 100 percent saints in public office, but you don't get all devils either! The point is, whether it's democracy or dictatorship, the system is good or evil depending on the men who run it. Evil men will use any system for evil purposes, and nobody disputes the fact that this is happening to our system today.

The answer is not to change the system, but to change the men who run it. Good men will use the system for benevolent purposes. Jesus Christ said,

> *The greatest among you will be your servant.* —Matthew 23:11

 Thursday

Revolutionary and radical are contradictory terms. Christ was not revolutionary. Christ was radical! He loved; He forgave; He sacrificed Himself for the sake of reconciliation. He abhorred alienation! Jesus Christ's way is not revolution; Jesus Christ's way is not repression. Jesus Christ's way is reconciliation!

Love and forgiveness are the desperate needs of our tragically polarized world. Where is the one who will love? Where is the one who will forgive?

"How often should I forgive?" asked Peter. "Seven times?" (He was self-impressed with his magnanimity, for the law required only three times.) "Not seven times," said Jesus, "but seventy times seven." Which is to say forgive to infinity, forgive as often as one sins against you, forgive every time!

Abhor and reject the vindictive spirit. Who dares to love? Who is strong enough to forgive?

> *Love your enemies and pray for those who persecute you.* —Matthew 5:44

 Friday

Labels! The way of the non-thinker. The way of the non-listener. The way of the closed mind. The lazy way!

Pin a label on a man and you can put your mind in neutral when he speaks. You don't even have to listen—just react automatically! Spot him as a liberal or conservative or moderate or radical or reactionary and that settles it—forever!

Some news commentators work this way: get a public figure pigeonholed and they can stop listening, stop thinking when he speaks. They interpret whatever he says in terms of their label, then rap out cliches which conform.

Ironically and tragically, many Christians use the label system. Once they get a man in a theological category, they never let him change. He's locked in for life! Dialogue is out; the best they can do is monologue at one another. As someone has put it, "Don't confuse me with the facts; I've already made up my mind." Christ's way is the way of change. He leaves room for a man to change and animates change in the man. Give a man growing room!

Do not judge, or you too will be judged.
—Matthew 7:1

 Monday

It's not easy to tell a Christian man from a non-Christian in America! In the first place, outward appearances are deceptive. They don't tell the whole story. A man can behave nicely for wicked reasons. One is not in a position to judge until all the facts are in; partial evidence is not adequate. But more important than this, outward signs do not necessarily indicate Christian character. Christianity is the moral and ethical norm in America. The average American, whether he claims to be a Christian or not, is more or less guided by Judeo-Christian standards. Brought up in the average home, attending the average school, he is bound to come under the influence of Christian teaching in spite of himself. With the result that even the raw pagan (in the biblical sense) living in America will order his life along Christian lines. Consequently we have a familiar phenomenon: the good man whose conduct is Christian but whose heart is not. Outwardly he acts like a Christian, yet he has no interest in Christ's church, much less any loyalty or personal attachment for Jesus Christ Himself.

As a matter of fact there is a distinct, basic difference between a Christian and a merely good man. It is an inner difference! The truly Christian man has a completely different outlook on life. He has a strong sense of obligation to God. The non-Christian does not feel this but rather feels self-made. The Christian believes himself to be a sinner saved by grace. The non-Christian does not feel he is a sinner, or if he does, he figures he can work his own way out of it. Hence the Christian sees Christ as Savior and Lord while the non-Christian sees Him merely as a good man or a great teacher. The Christian worships Christ. The non-Christian at best admires Christ, may even patronize Him. The Christian gives priority to the kingdom of God and its righteousness. The non-Christian never thinks of this. He is motivated by self-interest! Even the philanthropy of the non-Christian has a self reference. He wants credit for it. The Christian handles his resources as a steward of God. The non-Christian has the attitude of a squatter. The Christian gives God first place in financial considerations. The non-Christian figures he owns what he has: he's made it! Nobody, not even God, dictates how he'll use it! Self is at the center of the non-Christian's life, no matter how thoroughly he embraces Christian ethics. Jesus Christ is the center of the Christian's life. The Christian and non-Christian are at opposite poles when the secrets of their hearts are exposed!

> *Now this is eternal life: that men may know you, the only true God, and Jesus Christ, whom you have sent.*
> —John 17:3

 Tuesday

There could be a hundred million new Christians in the world today—one hundred million new converts to Jesus Christ—if just one in every nine professing Christians was really interested in winning a friend to Christ. One hundred million persons might be born into the Christian family through the power of God today, translated by the heart-changing dynamic of the Gospel from darkness to light, out of death into life—if one-ninth of us who claim to be Christian were really faithful followers of the One who said, "Follow me and I will make you fishers of men."

Of course you don't regiment the Spirit of God, and it is He who gives birth to the children of God. You don't dictate to God, setting quotas or schedules for the harvest of souls. Nevertheless, the statistics dramatize the thrilling possibilities of one day, any day, if we Christians were really serious about the mission to which our Lord has called us. Who can measure what the Spirit of God might do today if we who make profession of faith in Jesus Christ were obedient to the mandate which He left His church? What an absolutely exciting prospect if today each of us decided it was his duty, his vocation, his holy calling, to be a witness—by the Spirit—among his colleagues, friends, and associates.

Certainly the failure is not God's! It is "not His will that any should perish." He who loved the world so much that "He gave His one and only Son" is certainly not indifferent to the lostness, the waywardness, the disorientation of men. He who loved the world so much that He laid down His life on the cross, submitting to the ignominious treatment and shame of ruthless and profane men, letting His own blood pour out as a sacrifice for the sin of the very men guilty of the atrocity—surely He is not without care and concern for men everywhere. Surely He would speak to the hearts of men, woo them to Himself, if He had a faithful servant through whom to speak and love.

Jesus Christ has His people everywhere! But many are indifferent. They are cold and heartless and preoccupied with their own achievements and acquisitions. You aren't responsible for the nine hundred million who call themselves Christian, but you are responsible for you—and those around you.

> *But you will receive power when the*
> *Holy Spirit comes on you; and you will*
> *be my witnesses in Jerusalem, and all*
> *Judea and Samaria, and to the ends of*
> *the earth.* —Acts 1:8

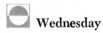 **Wednesday**

In a very real sense Christian witness is a secret service. The Christian who takes seriously his duty to God and man, who desires to exert a positive and constructive influence for Christ where he lives, has no infallible criteria whereby he may know how he is doing. In fact, those most deeply influenced by him may not be aware of that influence in the process. As the sun can tan a body without the conscious awareness of the one being tanned, so the godly influence of a thoughtful Christian may sink in and affect other lives without their knowledge. And the serious Christian is not aware of the transmission of his influence. He is just being himself, committed to Christ, dependent upon the Holy Spirit.

Today, in a hundred million places around the world, Christ-possessed Christ-filled persons will go quietly to their tasks and places in society, and throughout the day they will be permeating that society like a "benevolent infection" with Christian influence. They will not advertise, will not sound a trumpet before them, may not even talk a lot about it. They will not preach, will not "evangelize" in the conventional sense; but they will be a sermon. Their lives will "witness" to the reality and relevance of Christ. Today, parliaments, offices, schools and campuses, labor unions, military installations, clubs, markets, and homes all over the world will be silently infiltrated by faithful Christians whose lives, managed by the Holy Spirit, will bless and sweeten and challenge and preserve the little world in which they move. This is the heart and soul of the impact of the church in the world. This is the cutting edge, the point of thrust, the central impact of authentic Christian witness and influence as it penetrates the secular system.

Jesus said, "You are the salt of the earth." Salt is useless as long as it retains its identity in the salt shaker; only as it is spread on the food, losing its identity as it disappears, does it enhance and make palatable and preserve. So faithful Christians, "rubbed" by Christ into the society around them, disappear as they dissolve into that secular structure. And there, daily, they enhance and make palatable and preserve and make men thirsty for God and righteousness. Bless you, salt of the earth!

> *You are the salt of the earth. But if the salt loses its saltiness, how can it be made salty again? It is no longer good for anything, except to be thrown out and trampled by men.* —Matthew 5:13

 Thursday

The fruit of the teaching is the test of the teacher. It is one thing to take an academic interest in religion, any religion, far from the culture it produces; it is another to live in the environment the religion creates and perpetuates. It is easy enough to patronize a religion when one is an observer rather than an authentic participant; easy enough while one enjoys the bountiful benefits of a Judeo-Christian culture to be a proponent of a religion about which one has only theoretical

232

knowledge. It is easy to forget our heritage, take its priceless benefits for granted, and ignore the source from which they come.

But spend some time in a non-Christian environment where even simple cleanliness is a rare treasure and one begins to realize things are as they are, not in spite of the non-Christian religion, but because of it. Complacency, indifference to dirt and misery and suffering, filth, total absence of incentive, cheapness of life, unimportance of the individual, exploitation, corruption, superstition, etc. These are the status quo in a world without the influence of the Bible.

Whereas the great humanitarian benefits—hospitals, schools, hygiene, individual dignity, social welfare, orphanages, leprosariums—derive directly or indirectly from the Judeo-Christian tradition. Either they are the result of Christian nationals or foreign missions, or they are borrowed by imitation from the Christian world. Lean, hungry, sore-infested dogs, spit and vermin and dung; children with running noses, matted hair, open sores and scabs and scars, watery eyes; people bathing, washing dishes and clothes, brushing their teeth, swimming and excreting in the same river from which they get their drinking water; pathetic, abandoned old people; broken distorted bodies; and some will say, "They have their religion. Why should we send missionaries?" What terrible parasites are we who enjoy all the benefits of a Christ-generated civilization, yet reject

Him whose redemptive love produced the climate in which those benefits thrive and ignore the need and want of others!

> *Beware lest you say in your heart, "My power and the might of my hand have gotten me this wealth." You shall remember the Lord your God, for it is he who gives you power to get wealth.*
> —Deuteronomy 8:17-18

 Friday

"A pill to make sex safe."

That statement, from a contemporary best seller, expresses the ultimate in human selfishness, license, and irresponsibility. Followed to its logical conclusion, it would mean the end of the human family. It is to take the profoundest, most intimate, most deeply selfless, most meaningful, most personal human relationship and pervert it for utterly selfish, totally physical purposes. It is idolatry in its most subtle, most devastating form!

Sex is God's idea; created to give man his greatest pleasure, thereby guaranteeing the perpetuation of humanity; so constituted to give maximum satisfaction only when it is an exclusive relationship between one man and one woman committed to each other for life. It was intended to be the ultimate in self-surrender of a lover to his beloved and she to him.

Sex on any other basis is a will-o'-the-wisp, promising ecstasy and never really fulfilling, substituting animal pleasure for human commitment and surrender. The pay-off is sex purely as a technique: fail to get satisfaction, read another book, experiment with a new technique, use the sex partner like a guinea pig. That's exploitation of personality at its ugliest worst! That's sex without love!

How wonderfully, joyfully, gloriously different is God's plan. "Then the Lord God said, 'It is not good that the man should be alone. I will make him a helper.' ... (he) brought her to the man. Then the man said, "This at last is bone of my bones and flesh of my flesh" (Gen. 2:18, 22-23).

> *Therefore a man leaves his father and his mother and cleaves to his wife, and they become one flesh.* —Genesis 2:24

 Monday

The incredible fact of the Jew! Have you ever thought it through? The Jew is one of the strongest evidences for a personal God persevering in history to bring to pass His own eternal purpose. History is His-story! Begun with Abraham, two thousand years before Christ, the Jews have been dispersed and enslaved time after time in history, yet never obliterated. Disappearing from history as a nation six hundred years before Christ, persecuted generation after generation by some of the most fiendish and contemptibly cruel pogroms (consider the destiny of those nations which persecuted Jews); reappearing as a nation twenty-five centuries later, prospering and rising to international significance in twenty years!

Centuries before Christ, in the midst of rawest paganism, the Jew preserved the purest form of monotheistic religion with the highest ethical standards. From the Jew came the Ten Commandments, the most precise and comprehensive statement of moral law ever formulated. Think of the art and science and music the Jew has given to mankind. Think of the financial genius the Jew has given the world. The three great revolutions with which our modern world is wrestling were born of three Jews: Karl Marx precipitated the politico-economic revolution which is the focus of the present world crisis; Albert Einstein triggered the scientific revolution which may decide the progress of civilization, or its incineration; and Jesus Christ brought the spiritual and moral revolution upon which hangs the eternal destiny of humanity.

From Abraham to modern Israel; from Jerusalem under King David to Jerusalem under Golda Meir; the continuity of the Jew argues for the trustworthiness of the Bible, the validity of the Judeo-Christian tradition, the relevance of Christian faith. Let any man who would ignore the Bible or reject the faith of our Lord and Savior Jesus Christ give some intelligent thought to the incredible phenomenon of the Jew!

Salvation is from the Jews!   —John 4:22

 Tuesday

Corporate guilt is an illusion! The only relief is to the one who is imposing it, for the prophet seems to exclude himself from the indictment. By blaming everyone else he's home and free; his blanket accusation salves his own conscience. He may even feel he's a hero, daring to take such a bold stand against society in general.

Actually corporate responsibility is meaningless. People feel responsible individually or not at all. To be sure, responsible persons identify with other responsible persons and thus assume responsibility corporately; but as soon as individuals within such a collective lose their sense of responsibility, the whole structure weakens. The only ones who take corporate guilt seriously are those who suffer personal guilt; those not bothered by personal guilt couldn't care less. Corporate guilt gives them a perfect opportunity to cop out!

For the thoughtful person there's no way out of corporate guilt. He may regret his failure, his prejudice, his sin, and attempt to do something about it, but he finds no relief, for the prophet of doom, painting everybody with the same brush, includes him in his relentless blanket condemnation. God promises to forgive and bless a repentant nation, but repentance itself is a one-by-one proposition. Apart from individual repentance there is no corporate forgiveness and renewal. Persisting in the accusation of corporate guilt finally immobilizes a society because there is no way for the individual to respond and there is no other way society can respond to any challenge except individually. Perpetrating social guilt is futile!

> *If my people who are called by my name humble themselves, and pray and seek my face, and turn from their wicked ways, then I will hear from heaven, and will forgive their sin and heal their land.*
> —2 Chronicles 7:14

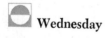 **Wednesday**

Three ways (at least) men use Scripture: some

use it as a collection of proof texts to support what they believe. They develop their theology, usually out of personal experience, then find Scripture to support their views. They suffer the false security that their belief is biblical whereas it may be unscriptural or even contradictory to the Bible. Experience, not the Bible, is their final authority. They learn little from the Scriptures, but search for texts to prove what they already hold to be true.

Others use Scripture as the starting point of their faith, from which they soon depart on their spiritual journey. The farther they go in their quest for spirituality, the farther they remove from their biblical beginning. Often they boast of a biblical faith when, as a matter of fact, their faith is biblical only in its genesis.

To others, Scripture is the foundation and the superstructure upon which and with which they build faith, "line upon line, precept upon precept."

The first group, using Scripture to their own subjective ends, develop an experience-centered faith which is tragically vulnerable because it is so helplessly dependent upon a sustained experience. The second group move horizontally from the Bible, generally boast of their orthodoxy, while the reality of biblical faith dims and dies. The third group move vertically and more deeply into Scripture, depend upon it for their sustenance, faith, and knowledge. Their confidence is based upon the Bible itself. The Bible becomes their meat and drink, their direction and goal, their teacher and motivator.

> *And he said to them, "You have a fine way of setting aside the commands of God in order to observe your own traditions."* —Mark 7:9

 Thursday

You've got one life. What are you doing with it? One life to live, one life to give. What are you living for? To what are you giving your life? Either you give your life to something, or you give it to nothing. In any case, you give it!

What consummate tragedy—good men who give their lives for nothing. Waste their lives on that which is temporary and transient when they could be investing their lives in that which is eternal. Good men they are too, but good for what? What a pity that there are men who are good, but good for nothing!

This is the greatest option in life: the privilege of giving your life to the highest and best or settling for the lowest and cheapest. Think of the men you know who have invested the best life has given them in that which has no significance in the light of eternity. They put all their eggs into the basket of life this side of the grave, and the payoff is disillusionment, frustration, boredom, and emptiness. They achieve everything they fight for and get nothing they really want. Everything turns to ashes in the sunset of life. They have everything they want and want little that they get.

> *My people have committed two evils;*
> *they have forsaken me, the fountain of*
> *living waters, and hewed out cisterns for*
> *themselves, broken cisterns, that can hold*
> *no water.* —Jeremiah 2:13

 Friday

The Christian hope is retroactive! Unlike all man-made utopias, its promise is relevant to those who have lived in past generations. Communism, for example, holds out no hope for Abraham, progenitor of Israel, who lived two thousand years before Christ. But Christianity does! In fact, Christianity, rightly understood, is the fulfillment of Abraham's hope.

The promise God made to Abraham (Gen. 12), two thousand years before Christ, is coming to its consummation and fulfillment in Jesus Christ. Every man who had faith in the God of Israel, from Abraham to Christ, is included in that promise and that hope! And the Apostle Paul declared (Rom. 8:18-23) that the whole created universe stands to benefit.

It is not uncommon for men to lay down their lives for one human dream or another, but apart from the heroism which is admirable, the dream will never pay off for the man who laid down his life. The most that he could hope for was that his posterity would enjoy the legacy left by his sacrifice. Every man who has sacrificed his life for the Christian "dream" is going to "collect" on the benefits, though he may have been dead a thousand years.

God began something with Adam, the first man (Gen. 2), which He is still working out in history. That plan, relevant not only to Adam but to the entire cosmos, will be consummated the day Jesus Christ makes His Second Advent on earth. He came once as a "suffering servant" to lay down His life on the cross for the sins of mankind. He is coming a second time as a conquering King to bring to fruition all the glorious prospects promised in the plan God began with Adam. All the legitimate dreams and aspirations of mankind from its beginning will find their perfection and fulfillment in Christ's return.

Creation itself will be liberated from its bondage to decay and brought into the glorious freedom of the children of God.
—Romans 8:21

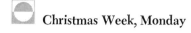

Peace wears different costumes: it may be real or an illusion! The peace of ignorance, for instance: one may have peace simply because he is uninformed; not knowing the facts, he remains undisturbed. "Ignorance is bliss." Or the peace of mental gymnastics: one pretends things are not as they are or actually convinces himself contrary to the truth like an ostrich with head in sand. There is the peace of fatalism: "What will be will be." Neither God (if there be a God) nor man can change inexorable, inflexible destiny. Such peace dooms a man to helplessness, feeds apathy, makes man a vegetable. It is also a beautiful defense for laziness. Then there is the peace of anesthesia, making one insensitive to reality. It may be induced by dope, liquor, or a mad whirl of pleasure; or one may just get very busy. This is the peace of escape. In one way or another some do whatever is necessary to remain numb to reality. All such peace is not only illusion, but it can be very dangerous! Like a "high threshold of pain" is dangerous. If a man doesn't feel pain, he will be indifferent to its cause. And he may be destroyed by it!

The peace of God is the only authentic peace! It works with things as they are! Apart from Jesus Christ, a man has two alternatives when faced with cold, hard facts: anxiety or false security.

Either he lets himself be distracted by trouble or he takes refuge in unreality. False peace disarms, puts one at the mercy of the facts. The peace of God mobilizes, enables one to keep his equilibrium in the face of the facts; makes him poised, efficient, capable. He is the master, never the victim, of circumstances. He is aware of the facts, but He is more than a match for them in the strength of Christ. He enjoys the genuine "undisturbedness" of the Lord Jesus. Such peace the world cannot give, and it cannot take it away either!

> *Do not let your hearts be troubled. Trust in God; trust also in me.* —John 14:1
> (See Philippians 4:6-7.)

 Christmas Week, Tuesday

Christmas has a carry-over, a follow-through. In fact that is the most important thing about it! If you have really kept Christmas, the joy of it has only begun. It is not meant to be a once-a-year spree or spasm; God meant it quite differently. Christmas is the beginning of God's program, just the beginning. And if you have really kept Christmas, then things have just begun for you. Do you keep Christmas or just observe the day? There is a vast difference!

Observing Christmas day is a cursory thing—momentary frills, tinsel, a flash-in-the-pan sort of thing. It's shallow, unreal, and exhausting. When it's over it's over. And frankly, people who just celebrate the day are relieved that it is over. They can return to normal; by which they mean that they can get back into the same old rut! But if you know the real meaning of Christmas, it is infinitely more than a mere celebration; it is a realization. It is not exhausting; it is transforming. It is a new birth! That's what it meant in the first place. Literally! It meant a new birth: the advent of God, in human form, in the Person of Jesus Christ into the world, into human affairs, human problems.

The birth of Jesus Christ into this world was only the beginning. The fundamental meaning of Christmas is that God demonstrated His interest, His concern for us, His love—a love that led to action. Love that led God to do something about man's need. It means that God desires to be born in the hearts of men everywhere: "God so loved the world that he gave his one and only Son."

God loved and gave, but we don't receive. That's the crux of our need! There's simply not a problem which touches our life in which God is not interested. He is a Father. His love is personal, practical, down-to-earth, realistic, available, continual, dependable.

Santa Claus is a usurper and the celebration an evil if it has no lasting effect in one's life—if we haven't Christmas in our heart. "Christ in you is the hope of glory." Not until Christ is in you can He help you. God had to enter the world to help it; He has to get into your heart to help you. Until you let Christ in, Christmas is a travesty, a fairy tale, a mockery, quiet blasphemy!

To all who received him . . . he gave the right to become children of God.
—John 1:12

 Christmas Week, Wednesday

"Peace on earth—among men of good will." That's the promise of Christmas! And what peace! It surpasses the ability of words to express or imagination to conceive. Paul describes it as "The peace which transcends all understanding." It is the legacy of those who take the promise of Christmas seriously.

There are many kinds of peace: the peace of ignorance, for example. As the saying goes, "Ignorance is bliss." Some people are at peace simply because they don't know any better; they are uninformed. No news is good news for them, and they would prefer to remain in their ignorance rather than have their peace disturbed. Then there is the peace of the sepulchre, the peace of apathy and inertia and indifference. "Couldn't care less" is its slogan, irresponsibility its hallmark.

But the peace of Christmas is the antithesis. It means peace whatever the news, however deeply one is involved, no matter how contrary the circumstances. It is a peace which helps a person fulfill responsibility efficiently and effectively. "An island of tranquillity at the center of my soul," is the way one young person described it recently. Circumstances were difficult, but a force within kept her steady and cool, like a giant gyroscope in the bowels of a great ship keeps it sailing smoothly however rough the seas.

The peace of Christmas at the center of one's life maintains the equilibrium despite swirling, turbulent, stormy circumstances. It is the antidote for fear, panic, and hysteria! It is the gift of God. Receive it this Christmas! You'll find it offered in Jesus Christ.

He himself is our peace.
—Ephesians 2:14

 Christmas Week, Thursday

Christmas is over. Its impact on the world staggers one. It is really amazing when you stop to think about it—the fuss the world makes over a baby born in a barn nineteen centuries ago. Christmas Eve, most of that day—in fact for several days preceding it—hour after hour over radio and television, as well as in newspapers and magazines, we are reminded of the strange fascination the birth of that babe holds for the whole world. The finest talent of art and music and literature, of the stage and screen, seem almost to vie with one another to portray this disarmingly simple event of history. No human power could perpetuate that kind of reverence and respect for such a humble event. No gimmick that Madison Avenue could think up today could promote such perennial excitement and adoration world-wide. (To be sure they do their best to capitalize on it.)

Why this universal focus on such an unpretentious fact of history occurring as it did in relative obscurity? Have you ever asked yourself that question? Ever wondered? What is there about the birth of a Jewish baby in a little suburb of Jerusalem, half a dozen miles from the civic center? Rome hardly noticed. Still today, nineteen hundred years later, its celebration is felt universally, even inspires a truce between warring nations. The answer to that question is that the birth of Jesus was tied into two thousand years of Hebrew history. God's promise to Abraham, progenitor of Israel, made 2000 B.C., was about to enter its most significant phase. The Messiah promised so long ago was about to enter history in supreme redemptive strategy. Two thousand years of history were about to see fulfillment! Two thousand years of anticipation, hope, aspiration, were to be satisfied. That is why Dr. Charles Malik, eminent Lebanese statesman, refers to Jesus Christ as "the hinge of history."

> *Do not be afraid. I bring you good news of great joy that will be for all people. Today in the town of David a Savior has been born to you; he is Christ the Lord.*
> —Luke 2:10-11

 Christmas Week, Friday

Indignation rose within me as I returned home from our Christmas day service. The golf course across the street was busy, and I wondered how many golfers were merchants or suppliers who had realized a neat profit from the Christmas trade. Impatient for Thanksgiving to be over (many could not wait), they had gone all out on their Christmas drives. The crowds came and the money poured in—all because "God so loved the world that he gave his one and only Son."

Many who prospered couldn't care less. They had exploited a Christian festival, gotten all they could out of it; now it was over, they had made their pile, and they hadn't the slightest thought for the One who made it possible. Not a moment's notice to God's gift! In total indifference to the Son of God whose birthday generated the sales, they ignored His church on Christmas day.

> *Take care lest you forget the Lord your God when you have eaten your fill, and have built fine houses to live in, and your silver and gold have increased, and everything you own has prospered, beware lest your heart grow haughty and you forget the Lord your God, and you say to yourselves, "My own power and might of my own hand have won this wealth for me." Remember that it is the Lord your God Who gives you the power to get wealth. If you do forget the Lord your God, I warn you this day that you shall certainly perish.* —The Torah
> (Deuteronomy 8:11-20)

 Easter Week, Monday

It is always too soon to quit! A man may quit because he feels the thing he's doing is not worth finishing. What he's doing may not be important, but he is. It's what quitting will do to him that matters. Inspiration gone? The excitement and idealism with which the project began has faded? Finishing doesn't seem worth the effort? Who cares? Maybe it doesn't make any difference to others if he quits, but it will make a great difference to himself; he's learning to be a quitter. It will be easier to quit next time. When things go stale, after the inspiration is gone, that is the time to dig in and finish the job simply for the sake of finishing.

Progress is made by the men who see a thing through after the quitters have dropped out. Jesus Christ is the supreme example. He went all the way to the cross, "set His face like a flint" to suffer crucifixion. He finished the work God gave Him to do and gave the world its ultimate hope! In that finish is God's complete forgiveness— eternal life for all who will receive it. Jesus said,

They (men) should always pray and not give up. —Luke 18:1

 Easter Week, Tuesday

Much social action, so far as goals are concerned, denies the very human dignity by which it professes to be motivated, for it is wholly materialistic. Its rationale is the good of man this

side of the grave. And if man has no eternal value, man is not man!

If all man's hope lies this side of death, man is hopeless and "most to be pitied." If there is nothing beyond the grave, morality is an illusion. Why be good when so many evil men prosper? And so many good people suffer?

What of the millions who have perished, who knew nothing but poverty while they lived? What of the millions whom life has cheated by cruel disease, by accident, by tragedy?

If there is no life beyond the grave, the death of Jesus Christ was wasted; the Resurrection of Christ was a cruel deception. Peter and Paul and the others were liars! If the grave is the end, eat, drink, and be merry, for tomorrow we die!

> *But Christ has indeed been raised from the dead!* —1 Corinthians 15:20

 Easter Week, Wednesday

God is dead? That's a contradiction in terms, like saying white is black, or love is hate, or straight is crooked, or light is darkness. That's like saying that life is dead!

The god of man's imagination is dead: the god we invent with our intellects, the god we insist on equating with our dogma, the god who is small enough for us to comprehend is dead; he's never been alive. The god we keep in a theological box is dead! But God is not dead! God is deathless! He is life itself. He is eternal. He is the great "I Am"!

He ever was and ever shall be. He is "the same yesterday, today and forever." He is the unchanging, unbegun, unending, perpetual Father of whom Jesus Christ is the only unchanging, unbegun, unending Son. He is the One who suffered profoundly, patiently when His Son hung on the cross. He was there to raise Him from the dead. The "God-is-dead" idea is a theory, a man-made theory, a human invention as irrelevant (as dead) as all the other theories about God, however sophisticated, conceived by man's intellect. We all tend to whittle God down to superman size by our dogma, but this is the absurd ultimate to which man's intellect leads in the reduction of God.

Who is this that darkens counsel by words without knowledge? —Job 38:2

 Easter Week, Thursday

Where was the body? Jesus' enemies would

have paid any price to recover it, for that would settle once for all Jesus' incredible claim that He would rise from the dead, and it would silence permanently His disciples. But their only recourse was to pay the guards to perjure themselves. And what a lie! "While they slept the disciples stole the body." If they were asleep, how did they know? (In their futile efforts to discredit the Resurrection, scholars have never fabricated a more satisfactory explanation.)

Jesus' enemies, remembering His promise to rise from the dead, took every precaution to prevent it, actual or contrived. Three days later the seal was broken, the stone rolled away, the body gone. The burial linen remained in the tomb like a cocoon.

For six weeks Jesus revealed Himself time and again in ways which left no doubt whatsoever that He was alive (see 1 Cor. 15:5-8). His disciples did not convince easily! They thought He was a ghost. He invited them to handle His body; He partook of their food. Thomas refused to believe unless He could feel the wounds of the nails and spear. Jesus submitted to Thomas's test leaving Thomas with no doubts. Jesus even prepared a breakfast and dined with His disciples (John 21:9-12).

It is inconceivable that the disciples tricked the guards, stole the body, buried it in an unknown grave, waited fifty days for a cooling-off period, and then, in spite of every kind of threat and intimidation, preached the Resurrection with conviction and power. That is more difficult to accept than the Resurrection itself! Nor is it conceivable that the church, generation by generation, for nineteen centuries, has been deluded in its testimony to the Resurrection. Easter Sunday may be perfunctory to many, but to millions it is the celebration of an historical fact which has been confirmed in personal experience.

After his suffering, he showed himself to these men and gave many convincing proofs that he was alive. —Acts 1:3

 Easter Week, Friday

It is certainly not missing the mark to say that Jesus was the most captivating, the most fascinating personality who ever walked the earth. The record of His life indicates that there was a magnetism about Him that drew great crowds. During His brief ministry, He was hardly ever free from the multitudes, even when He deliberately avoided them and sought isolation. His fame spread to the four corners of Palestine: "No man ever spoke like this man," they said of Him. "He speaks as one having authority. From whence has this man such learning?" they inquired.

Whence this magnetism, this irresistible attraction, this power of word? It is an open secret. He did not hesitate to share it with those who were interested. He disclosed again and again the source of His powerful ministry. He said His words were not His own, but His Father's. He insisted His works were not his own but the Father's. The Father spoke the word and did the work through Him by the agency of the indwelling Holy Spirit. Jesus Christ the man was strictly obedient to the Father's will—and filled with the Spirit of God (Luke 4:1). Before Jesus ascended following His Resurrection, He promised to His disciples the same Spirit who had filled His life and employed Him to do the will of the Father. On the basis of this promise He was able to say to His disciples, "Anyone who has faith in me will do what I have been doing. He will do even greater things than these" (John 14:12).

Fifty days after Passover came Pentecost. At Pentecost every disciple of Jesus was "filled with the Spirit of God," and that loose band of individualistic disciples was forged into an absolutely unique and unprecedented social unit—the church, the Body of Christ.

Be filled with the Spirit. —Ephesians 5:18